RELIGION AND SOCIAL JUSTICE

Religion and Social Justice

Shivesh C. Thakur
Professor of Philosophy
University of Northern Iowa

First published in Great Britain 1996 by
MACMILLAN PRESS LTD
Houndmills, Basingstoke, Hampshire RG21 6XS
and London
Companies and representatives
throughout the world

A catalogue record for this book is available
from the British Library.

This book is published in Macmillan's *Library of Philosophy and Religion*
Series editor: John Hick

ISBN 0–333–60990–5

 First published in the United States of America 1996 by
ST. MARTIN'S PRESS, INC.,
Scholarly and Reference Division,
175 Fifth Avenue,
New York, N.Y. 10010

ISBN 0–312–15936–6

Library of Congress Cataloging-in-Publication Data
Thakur, Shivesh Chandra.
Religion and social justice / Shivesh C. Thakur.
  p.   cm. — (Library of philosophy and religion (Houndmills,
Basingstoke, England))
Includes bibliographical references and index.
ISBN 0–312–15936–6
1. Religion and justice.   2. Social justice.   I. Title.
II. Series.
BL65.J87T43   1996
291.1'78—dc20   96–7683
                                                     CIP

10   9   8   7   6   5   4   3   2   1
05 04 03 02 01 00 99 98 97 96

Printed and bound in Great Britain by
Antony Rowe Ltd, Chippenham, Wiltshire

Contents

Preface

The material constituting this book was put together over a number of years, some of its chapters originally forming the basis for lectures given at various professional gatherings, some published as articles in journals or anthologies. Chapter 4 is a copy of my keynote address at a symposium on Religion and Social Justice, on the occasion of the annual conference of the Iowa Academy of Religion/Iowa Theological Conference, held at the University of Northern Iowa, in March 1985. Chapter 6 formed the basis of a public lecture on 'Religion, Economic Development and Social Justice: A View from the Moral Highground', given at the College of the Holy Cross, at Worcester, Massachusetts, in April 1987, and paraphrased at a symposium on Religion and Economics, sponsored by the Department of Religious Studies at the University of California at Santa Barbara, in April 1991. Chapter 7 represents the text of a public lecture given at the Philosophy and Religion Forum, at the University of Northern Iowa, in November 1993 (an earlier version of it having been presented at a symposium on Religion and Nationalism in South Asia, held at Santa Barbara, in April 1989). Although these pieces have been partly rewritten in the interests of the unity of this book, a conscious attempt has been made to keep them as close to the original as possible. That may help explain the slight differences in the tone and style of presentation of some of these chapters. It is appropriate at this point to mention two other essays. 'Just Society: God's Shadow or Man's Work?', was presented at a conference on 'God: the Contemporary Discussion' held in Seoul in August 1984 and published in *The Search for Faith and Justice in the Twentieth Century*, ed. Gene G. James (New York, 1987); and 'Social Justice: An Informal Analysis' was published in *International Philosophical Quarterly*, Vol. XXVI, no. 3, September 1986. The published articles, although on the theme of religion and social justice, have not, however, been included here, because their contents were deemed to be outside the scope of this book. But each of them gave rise to discussions from which I have profited greatly.

In the course of preparing and presenting these lectures/articles, not to mention the discussions with professional colleagues following the presentations, I learnt a lot from many different sources, too numerous even to remember now. To all of those sources of my learning, I offer grateful thanks. I acknowledge particular appreciation of my debts, in this regard, to my colleagues in the Department of Philosophy and Religion, here at the University of Northern Iowa, who have all helped, immeasurably, in many different ways – only some of them are acknowledged in the references. Among them, however, especially deserving of thanks are Edward Amend and William Clohesy, who looked at drafts of a chapter each and made valuable suggestions. While all of them helped towards improving the content and quality of the book, the deficiencies that remain – and there may be too many of them, I'm afraid – are entirely my own responsibility.

On a different note, I am grateful to the University of Northern Iowa for the award of a Professional Development Leave during 1992–93, which allowed me time to do the thinking and research needed for this book. Finally, computer-illiterate as I am, I could not possibly have put the typescript for this book together without the patient and hard work of Helen Harrington, the secretary of my department. To her I express my sincere and heartfelt thanks.

SHIVESH THAKUR
Cedar Falls

Introduction

To those who still cling to the belief, held by many nineteenth-century intellectuals, that religion was only a relic in the evolutionary history of humanity, this book may seem to be of merely theoretical interest, perhaps not even that. But their belief, it seems to me, has turned out to be contrary to fact. Writing even before the occurrence of the revolution in Iran ushered in by the late Ayatollah Khomeini in 1979, and its aftermath, Trevor Ling had this to say about the 'persistence of religion':

> Marx, like Auguste Comte and a number of other intellectuals in the nineteenth century, believed that wherever modern science and technology penetrated, religion was doomed. It might persist for a while, but it could have no real vitality left in the modern world; its last spasmodic strugglings would soon be ended and it would lie still.[1]

He concludes, justifiably, I believe, that *'such has not been the case'* (italics mine). Not only has it not been the case, but, on the contrary, religion has made an enormous come-back on the world's political and social stage, spurred, partly, at least, by the Khomeini revolution itself. So much so that by 1993, a major book devoted to the subject is able to claim that there may be a 'new cold war' between 'religious nationalism' and the 'secular state', replacing the old one between the democratic West and the communist states within the former Soviet bloc.[2] And this observation seems to be vindicated by the emergence right round the world of militant forms of religious nationalism and fundamentalism, just as much an actual and potential threat to peace and stability in the world as the old Cold War ever was. Furthermore, the very dissolution of the former Soviet Union and all that it stood for means that the socialist path of achieving social justice, namely, the revolutionary redistribution of wealth, has been discredited — at least for the foreseeable future. And liberalism, the other political alternative, has increasingly come under attack from communitarians and conservatives alike. These empirical facts make it particularly important to study the role of religion in social justice, although, I think, such a study has intrinsic worth, quite independently of these contingent phenomena.

A complex subject, like the overall relationship between religion and social justice naturally raises many different issues. Accordingly, I have a number of different claims to investigate, a number of questions to raise and not a few suggestions to make throughout this volume. But even at the risk of over-simplification, I ought to give readers, at the very outset, a reasonably clear idea of what the book is about and how I propose to achieve my goals. My main thesis, I would like to say, is that although religion should not be viewed as a direct instrument of social justice, it may have an enormous indirect role to play: perhaps it may even be a precondition of the latter. In other words, it is possible to argue that, in the absence of the absolute morality and spiritual vision that only religion can provide, social justice may be hard, if not impossible, to attain. I will try to show that this fact – if it is a fact – sets up not just a contingent or coincidental but, rather, a necessary and conceptual conflict between two rival utopias – the biblical idea of the kingdom of God (and its counterparts in the other 'great religions'), on the one hand, and the liberal vision of social justice, on the other. I hope to show that this conflict or tension, provided it does not lead to war or violence, may even be salutary. That is so because when religion and liberalism act as much-needed counterweights to each other, not only does each guard humanity against the excesses of the other, but this opposition also maximizes the conditions under which social justice can be attained.

This overall conclusion is reached through the examination of several issues, according to the following plan. Since 'social justice' is a subcategory of the broader concept, 'justice', and can hardly be understood apart from it, Chapter 1 discusses the language, vocabulary and context of justice generally, while, at the same time, outlining the broad contours of social justice. Chapter 2 introduces some philosophical theories of justice, concentrating especially on those to which the notion of social justice is central, namely, liberal and socialist theories. This plan has been adopted in the hope that even those not already familiar with the philosophical issues and technical terminology related to the concept of social justice, may be enabled to appreciate what is involved in the substantive questions discussed later in this book.

In a sense, Chapter 3 is also like Chapters 1 and 2, namely, intended to give readers familiarity with basic terms and views – in this case about the idea of justice in the great religions. But, at the same time, it is designed to provide an indirect argument against religion being construed as an instrument of social justice. That is done by showing that these religions have been concerned primarily with personal righteousness, and not with social justice in the distributive sense that the contemporary usage of this term has acquired. This chapter also introduces, although only briefly, the very potent biblical idea of the kingdom of God, and its nearest equivalents in the world's other great religions, without, however, discussing the implications of this idea at this stage. With the preliminaries thus over, the stage is set for a discussion of the substantive issues.

Chapter 4 raises some philosophical questions designed to show, in a general way, why it is a mistake to regard religion as a tool of social justice, the latter being a concept arising out of the liberal (and socialist) vision of humans and their place in the world. Chapter 5 outlines and examines Latin American 'Liberation theology', which explicitly avows that religion – at least, Christianity – is, and should be, an instrument of social justice in the world. The conclusion reached is that Liberation theology, whatever its motivation, is wrong in thinking that social justice should be the primary, if not the sole, goal of religion: this thinking, I claim, involves a misunderstanding of the proper role of religion. It is argued, further, that the political and economic collapse of the former communist states, based on Marxist dogma, discredits Liberation theology, as also, perhaps, the claims of all those who advocate Marxist revolutionary violence and class struggle as a means to social justice. If so, that leaves two contenders, or perhaps just one, in the field, claiming to be the agents of social justice; the capitalist model of economic development as its economic tool and the liberal theory of justice (and liberalism, generally) as its political tool. Since capitalism and liberalism are allies, one could say that there is only one contender left, with two arms, one economic and the other political. Withholding the discussion of liberalism until Chapter 10, Chapter 6 examines whether, to what extent, and within what limits, economic development may be a means to social justice. It also discusses what role, if any, religion could be said to have in economic development, and, indirectly, in bringing about social justice.

Chapter 7 looks at the two most important forms the recent resurgence of religion is taking, that is, religious nationalism and religious fundamentalism, and a case is made that, while these movements are generally allies, they are not identical. What the two invariably have in common, however, is their dislike, not so much of modernity, but of 'modernism', the individualism, secularism, hedonism, etc. underpinning the liberal democracies in the West today. Since the latter take the separation of religion and state for granted, this is one of the targets of attack by the religious militants; Chapter 8 examines afresh the relationship between religion and state (and, generally, between religion and politics and religion and public life). The conclusion reached is that, although this separation is not easy to maintain in practice, nevertheless it ought to be maintained for the benefit not just of the state, but of religion too.

In Chapter 9 the idea of the kingdom of God, introduced in Chapter 3, is picked out for a more detailed investigation, especially in relation to the question whether the prerequisites for the kingdom can be said to promote the picture of 'the good life' postulated by and practised in capitalist, affluent societies. Chapter 10 takes up an examination of the liberal theory of justice, and of liberalism generally, and tries to show that practically everything this ideology promotes, more particularly its ethic of rights, is antithetical to the religious view of the place of humans on earth, especially the ethic of duties that it incorporates. Finally, Chapter 11, the last of this book, concludes by drawing together the various theses of the book and arguing that the clash between the utopias, embedded in religion, on the one hand, and liberalism, on the other, may possibly be healthy for both and good for humankind.

1 Justice: A Preliminary Survey

'Social justice' is a sub-category of the broader concept, 'justice', and can hardly be understood apart from the latter. In this chapter, therefore, I talk largely about justice in general, while, at the same time, trying to outline the broad contours of social justice.

THE OBJECTS OF JUSTICE

That a sense of justice is a very important attribute of individuals as well as societies, is not a controversial claim. But controversy and disagreement arise instantly when we ask what precisely justice is. The adjective 'just' is used to characterize, primarily, persons and their acts. But people do talk – without any impropriety in language, I think – of just institutions or regimes, for example. John Rawls speaks of just 'institutions' and 'practices';[1] and David Miller not only talks of just 'states of affairs', but, in fact, thinks that this use must be regarded as the primary one.[2] Whether he is right or not, one thing seems clear: the objects of justice cover a wide range. Although we frequently make judgments about just people, acts, etc., usually, our judgments are prompted by our perception of *in*justice in them. In order, therefore, to get a preliminary idea of what justice might be, it may be useful to think of situations which we typically characterize as 'unjust'. A bank robber is an unjust person, because through his actions he is unfairly taking what does not belong to him. If I beat a person to death for hurling abuse, I am acting unjustly; for the punishment inflicted seems to be far in excess of the crime. If I hold that I ought to treat people in ways that I do not want to be treated myself, then I am advocating an unjust principle; for it seems to be lacking in considerations of reciprocity and fairness, marks of justice as well as of moral correctness. If an institution practises discrimination in employment on grounds of colour of skin or sex, it is not a just institution; for it is allowing irrelevant factors to decide who should be employed. A state of affairs is unjust if it encourages, permits or ignores unnecessary pain or hardship being suffered by a sentient being – human or non-human: our sense of justice is offended when we encounter or think of the suffering of the disabled or of the victims of an earthquake. For, as far as we can see, they have done nothing to deserve the suffering. Such a view can, for example, be taken if we think that the victims are being punished by supernatural powers for their supposed 'sins', which we ourselves, however, do not believe the victims to be guilty of. We are perpetrating injustice, again, if we distribute the products of a cooperative enterprise in such a way that some get too much and others too little, that is, when the reward is not in proportion to the effort of individuals. Injustice is also being perpetrated if we discover that certain individuals are coerced into sacrificing their own interests, even if the sacrifice is for a larger, in itself noble, cause. Nor is our sense of justice unruffled when we see that individuals or entire populations are starving or ill-nourished while others indulge in 'conspicuous consumption'. What makes all these diverse instances, and the many more that can no doubt be listed, instances of injustice? The only safe answer perhaps is that they all share an absence of 'fittingness'. But that is not saying very much. The question 'What is justice?' has merely been postponed, and now reappears as 'What is "fittingness"?'. Until we begin to discuss the details in this and the next chapter, there may not be much more to say, except to point out that justice has a great deal to do with 'fittingness', 'fairness', 'proportion', and so on.

THE CONTEXT OF JUSTICE

It is easy to see, if we just look at the few examples cited above, that only under certain broad conditions can questions of justice or injustice arise. Only sentient beings, for example, can inflict or suffer injustice. If I disfigure or destroy a valuable diamond, I am not being unjust to the stone, although I am behaving irrationally. But if I subject an animal to unnecessary cruelty, I am treating the animal unjustly. (If anyone has qualms about calling any treatment of animals just or unjust, I would like to remind them of those who insist that animals have rights.) However, if this animal were to bite, bruise, or even kill me, it could not be said to have treated me unjustly. This is because although all sentient beings can be said to *suffer* injustice, only a special sub-class of them can be said to *commit* injustices, namely, the sub-class or species of humans. For only the latter are regarded as rational. Non-rational sentient beings cannot be said to be capable of discriminating between just and unjust acts, or for that matter, of making judgments of any sort, and hence of acting justly or unjustly. Judgments of justice or injustice are moral judgments, whenever they are not merely legal; and since rationality is a pre-condition of morality, only a rational being can be just or unjust.

This connection of justice with morality also implies that the typical context of justice, like that of morality, is social. In a world inhabited by a single being, questions of justice or injustice would not arise, nor those of morality or immorality. But given the context of society, an individual may be judged to have, or to lack, principles, dispositions or habits which make for or militate against a just state of affairs in the society. Hence justice can be said to be the virtue of individuals as well as of societies.[3]

But while justice does have a social context, it is possible to imagine a society in which questions of justice or injustice would either not arise at all, or, if they did, would be purely 'academic'. As Rawls points out, an association of saints where no one ever inflicted, or even contemplated, an injury to another, or took away what was not one's own, or broke a promise or contract, would obviously not be a society where conflicts about justice or injustice could abound, or be important.[4] Similarly, we can follow Hume's suggestion and imagine a society in which justice would not be an important, or even useful, concept. Here are his words:

> Let us suppose that nature has bestowed on the human race such profuse *abundance* of the *external* conveniencies, that, without any uncertainty in the event, without any care or industry on our part, every individual finds himself fully provided with whatever his most voracious appetites can want, or luxurious imagination wish or desire. His natural beauty, we shall suppose, surpasses all acquired ornaments: The perpetual clemency of the seasons renders useless all cloaths or covering: The raw herbage affords him the most delicious fare; the clear fountain, the richest beverage. No laborious occupation required: No tillage: No navigation. Music, poetry, and contemplation, form his sole business: Conversation, mirth and friendship his sole amusement.
>
> It seems evident, that, in such a happy state, every other social virtue would flourish, and receive tenfold encrease; but the cautious, jealous virtue of justice would never once have been dreamed of. For what purpose make a partition of goods, where everyone has already more than enough? Why give rise to property, where there cannot possibly be any injury? Why call this object *mine*, when, upon the seizing of it by another, I need but stretch out my hand to possess myself of what is equally valuable? Justice, in that case, being totally USELESS, would be an idle ceremonial, and could never possibly have place in the catalogue of virtues.[5]

Also, if there were a society in which all members were friends, considerations of justice would not typically govern its affairs. For in such a society love, and not justice, would be the ruling force. Typically, therefore, the context of justice presupposes unfulfilled needs and wants, competition for scarce goods and resources, rivalry for rewards and privileges, and, very importantly, the urge to power and prestige. In other words, the more imperfect the world, the greater its need for justice.

KINDS OF JUSTICE

Some desirable clarity regarding the concept of justice may be obtained by distinguishing between various kinds, or senses, of justice. The following represent a few of these distinctions; but it ought to be noted that since the criteria of distinction used are not always mutually exclusive, some of the distinctions can be seen to be overlapping. We may thus distinguish between '*legal*' justice, on the one hand, and '*moral*' justice on the other. According to this classification, an act, practice or institution is just if it accords with the relevant law in existence; and a person is just in this sense if he obeys the law. But not every piece of legislation used need be morally justified. In certain societies, for example, polygamy is legal; but an individual, either within or outside that society, may deem that practice to be morally unjust, because in his/her opinion, it treats women unfairly. This is just one example of the ways in which law and morality, and, therefore, legal and moral justice may conflict.

A closely related, but different, distinction can be made between '*conservative*' and '*prosthetic*' or '*ideal*' justice.[6] The protection and continuation of an existing system of rights, rewards or privileges may be deemed to be natural and just; and, therefore, requiring to be maintained by law. But from a different point of view, we may wish to invoke an ideal system – which may never have existed – by contrast with which the existing system may seem to be unjust, and so, not deserving of legal protection and maintenance. While it is likely that conservative justice will, by and large, incorporate all or most of what we earlier called legal justice, that need not be the case: the former may well include practices that are quite conventional, but not legally sanctioned. Similarly, prosthetic or ideal justice may, but need not, incorporate only moral justice: it may well include religious ideals, for example, which may not fall within the limits of morality, strictly speaking. But it should, again, be noticed that the potential for conflict between conservative and ideal justice is quite significant.

Following Aristotle, it has been customary to distinguish between '*corrective*' and '*distributive*' justice.[7] The latter involves the distribution of economic goods, such as food, shelter, health-care, money, and so on, or rewards and privileges, such as honour, power, and so on, among members of a society, according to some principle(s) of justice. The former involves 'righting' the 'wrongs' in transactions between one individual and another, or between groups of individuals. These transactions themselves may include 'voluntary' ones, such as the sale and purchase of property, borrowing, lending, pledging, and so on, on the one hand; and 'involuntary' ones, such as theft, adultery, poisoning, assassination, false witness, assault, murder, robbery, imprisonment, and so on, on the other. The rectification or 'correction' appropriate in many of these instances of 'transactions' may well be punishment of one sort or another. And, insofar as that may be the case, an important question may arise as to the aim of punishment. Should the aim of punishment be revenge or retribution, as was customarily supposed by most traditional societies; or should it be the reform and rehabilitation of offenders? Depending on the answer one wishes to give to this question, punishment may be viewed as either *'retributive'* or *'reformative'*. To what extent should punishment be aimed at *'deterring'* either the same offender or another one from committing the same, or similar, offence in future, is a related but different question. Deterrence may be viewed either as an alternative to retribution and reform, or as an additional element in one or the other, or even both. It may be worth noting here that even if retribution is sanctioned by law as appropriate in the consideration of punishment, someone adopting a moral point of view may well regard it as morally unjust; and the ensuing debate, if there is one, on the merits of the competing views of punishment could very well still be a debate about justice in the larger sense.

Some authors distinguish between *'private'* and *'social'* justice;[8] and although justice cannot, strictly speaking, be private, this contrast is not altogether unhelpful, if only because it tends to bring to light yet another source of conflict between justice in its different senses, or settings. If a manufacturer, for example, decides to settle an actual or potential wage dispute with his employees by giving them very high wages, this private settlement need not normally be an outsider's concern at all. But if it gives rise to discontent and strife among workers doing similar work for other manufacturers who pay much lower wages, then the very positive action of the first employer – which is not only just, but generous – would seem to militate against social justice, across the board. It should be evident that this distinction only makes sense if one assumes an egalitarian principle of justice, namely, that equal or similar work deserves equal or similar pay, regardless of where one works.

That brings us, finally, to the distinction between *'individual'* and *'social'* justice. As we mentioned briefly, fairly early on, although justice has a necessarily social context, an individual may be – is – called just if he possesses those attributes, habits, or dispositions which are likely to contribute to justice in society, especially if he/she displays them invariably and uniformly in all his/her dealings with other members of society. It is for this reason that justice has been regarded as the virtue of an individual as well as of a society. Starting from the point of view of this particular contrast then, social justice could include all forms of justice – legal, moral, conservative, ideal, corrective and distributive – insofar as they apply to society. But a convention seems to have developed which restricts the application of the term 'social justice' primarily, to the second halves of the pairs of contrasts discussed earlier. It may, I think, be wise to call the former the wide sense of 'social justice' and the latter its conventional or narrow sense. As long as the context makes it clear in which of the two senses the term is being used on a given occasion, there should be nothing lost in retaining both senses. But, unfortunately, indiscriminate use of the phrase, without specifying its meaning, is not uncommon. There is no doubt, however, that 'social justice' has come to refer primarily to distributive justice, especially as it pertains to the distribution of economic goods and political status and power in society.

THE PRINCIPLES OF JUSTICE

By way of elucidation of the concept of justice, all we were able to say earlier was that it seems to have a great deal to do with 'fittingness', 'fairness' and 'proportion' etc. But any judgment of what is fitting, fair, or in due proportion presupposes that we have some principle(s) in mind in relation to which the action, practice, and so on, in question is to be judged as fair, etc. We are here confronting one of the most difficult and complex issues relating to justice: fair or fitting in respect of what? Clearly, one should expect, and there are, many answers. *At least* three, not always mutually compatible, principles stand out for consideration immediately: rights, deserts and needs. If we accept the conventional wisdom that doing justice means giving 'to each his due'[9] – and there seems to be no good reason why we should not – then we have to ask the further question as to what constitutes one's 'due'. And one may quite reasonably answer the question either in terms of rights, deserts or needs. What is 'due' to a person can almost equally plausibly be argued to be either whatever he has a right to, or whatever he deserves, or what he needs. If the consideration of one of these demanded a course of action which was always identical with that demanded by the other two, then, of course, there would be no problem. But that does not seem to be the case: the three are irreducibly distinct concepts, although it is always possible to have a situation in which what one needed was what one deserved as well as what one had a right to.

It is not wildly implausible to take the view that, in an ideal world at least, one would have a right to all one needed, and perhaps only to what one needed. This looks more plausible when negatively expressed: that is, no one should have a right to what one does not need; and no one should be denied the right to what he or she needs. It should not be difficult to see that this claim has already shifted the focus from conservative to ideal justice and from legal to moral justice. But once such a switch is made, the claim does not seem altogether revolutionary. Now, how about deservingness? It is certainly very reasonable to argue that in a humane and plentiful society one would deserve to have whatever one needs, or has a right to. And it does not take too much stretching to argue, besides, that in a non-hierarchical, egalitarian and cooperative society, where everyone is supposed to work according to the best of their ability, no one can be said to deserve what he/she does not have a right to, for in that case he/she presumably does not need it. As the Marxist dictum goes: 'from each according to his ability, to each according to his need'.[10] While argument and counter-argument of this sort can, and should, go on, it should be recognized that these are special arguments which depend on special theories of justice. Without recourse to these, it seems best to recognize the distinctness of the three concepts and to take the position that all of them are relevant principles of justice. Such a position, however, obliges one to accept the inevitability of the problems that arise regarding how best to balance these principles and decide, if this can be done in any formal or procedural way, what the relative priorities between them ought to be. There are enough problems lurking here already. But, still, why might not one add that what one should get is neither what one needs, or deserves, or has a right to but what is 'good' for one, in some unspecified, but specifiable, sense of 'good'? A 'paternalistic' conception of justice might indeed give rise to such a principle of distribution.

THEORIES OF JUSTICE

Theories of justice may be offered, or required, for various reasons. In the context of corrective justice, for instance, theories may be put forward arguing why retribution, reform or deterrence is or is not an appropriate goal of punishment, or proposing some principle entirely different from these three as the basis of punishment, or indeed arguing why *any* notion of punishment is contrary to the spirit of justice. When it comes to distributive justice, and more particularly what we earlier called the narrow sense of social justice, theories may be devised to delineate what the principles of distribution ought to be, or to elaborate a particular ordering of priorities among already recognized principles, such as rights, deserts and needs and so on, or to propose precise operational renderings of these very vague general principles. Three well-known types of such theories have become familiar in modern political philosophy: *Libertarian*, which in one form or another, propose that justice consists in securing and preserving the maximum possible liberty for all individuals and whatever distribution results from an efficient market economy, in which equality of opportunity exists; *Liberal*, which try to combine both liberty and social equality into one ultimate moral ideal, typically, stressing economic liberty and political equality; and *Socialist*, which insist on equal distribution of economic goods among all individuals and eschew individual privileges, including the right to ownership of private property, thus assigning the highest moral priority to social equality. Actual theories frequently turn out to be neither purely one nor the other, but contain mixtures of varying sorts of elements from the ideal types mentioned above, especially as they take positions regarding what form of government might best bring about the preferred kind of just social order.

TWO BROAD CLASSES OF THEORIES

The three types of theories of justice enumerated above, although the best known among modern ones, are not at all the only ones offered, even as theory-types, and even in recent times, not to mention the entire history of social and political thought. But these are, indeed, the prime examples of what, following Hans Kelsen,[11] I might call '*Rationalistic*' theories, as against those that he calls '*Metaphysical-religious*'. The distinction between these two very broad classes of theories – or of theory-types, if you will – rests on how each class of theories is justified. Rationalistic theories, whatever the differences among them, justify their concept of justice, its priority among other virtues, and its principles by claiming that they are the products of human reason. In other words, questions like 'Why should I be just?', or 'Why should this one, rather than some other, be regarded as a principle of justice?', are, typically answered by saying, or implying, that these are the dictates of human reason – certainly, of human reason under ideal conditions. This human reason may refer either to our capacity to think or reflect in a general way, or only to that part of it which allows us to recognize that we have desires or interests and enables us to determine under what conditions these interests may be best served. What rationalistic theories, in our present context, do not do is postulate or imply any metaphysical or religious entities, properties, virtues or processes whose existence could be required for the derivation of either the concept or the principles of justice.

Metaphysical-religious theories, on the other hand, do make such a postulation. Plato stands out as the kind of thinker for whom the ultimate justification for justice in this world is the fact that, in a world beyond this one, that is, in the world of Forms, there exists a Form of Justice. Perfect justice, like perfect beauty, is not to be found in this world; and what little there is of it here is so because it is a poor reflection of its 'master-original', the Form of Justice. This Form of Justice itself, however, is an integral part of the Form of the Good, the highest reality in Plato's scheme, comparable in many ways to the theistic idea of God. Needless to say that religions, in like fashion, provide justification for justice by claiming it to be an attribute of God, or of whatever it is that constitutes the ultimate fabric of reality. It is important to be just because we are God's children and He is just; or because justice is a component of the ultimate structure of reality and, therefore, cannot be ignored. Principles of justice are what they are because they are divine commands, representing God's rational will. And, according to some, for example, St Paul, human reason, even at its best, may not be able to fathom the mysteries of divine justice. Hence our utter dependence on scripture and the prophets and saints in deciphering the true meaning of justice.

According to Kelsen,[12] this division between the rationalistic and the metaphysical-religious applies even to the so-called Natural Law theories of justice which were proposed during the seventeenth and eighteenth centuries. Natural law theories regard justice to be an integral part of the constitution of nature in general, and of human nature in particular. Nature, thus, becomes a model of the laws of justice and order: by analyzing nature, we can discover the norms prescribing the just conduct of human beings. If nature is regarded as created by God, then the laws of nature are regarded as the expression of the will of God. If, however, natural law is regarded as being deducible from human reason alone, then there is no need to see it as rooted in any transcendental entities or processes. This latter version of natural law theories would, then, provide examples of what we called rationalistic theories of justice, whereas the former would illustrate its metaphysical-religious variant. Thus there is no good reason to think that natural law theories herald the breakdown of the division between the two broad classes of theories outlined at the beginning of this section.

All that needs to be added here is that Chapter 2 will discuss details of some of the rationalistic theories, and Chapter 3 those of the metaphysical-religious theories embedded in the great religions of the world.

2 Philosophical Conceptions of Justice

In this chapter I intend to discuss, primarily, those theories of justice referred to in the last chapter as liberal, libertarian and socialist. This is because these are the prime modern examples of what, towards the end of the last chapter, I characterized as rationalistic theories. As one would expect, these also happen to be the theories whose main preoccupation in the context of justice is what, in Chapter 1, I called the narrow sense of 'social justice', dealing primarily with questions of fair distribution of economic and political goods in society. As a useful prelude to the discussion of these theories, however, I include a brief reference to Aristotle. This is only partly because his views on justice can be safely regarded as of the rationalistic type, appealing as they do, not to any transcendental reality but to common-sense or human reason in decisions concerning questions of justice. This might have been enough of a reason for the inclusion of Aristotle here. But there are also two additional, but related, reasons. One of them is that it is to Aristotle that we owe some of our very important technical vocabulary and maxims relating to justice. But secondly, and more importantly, some of his distinctions and maxims, although formulated a long time ago, still have relevance, even if only as starting points; and references to Aristotle even by modern theorists of justice are not infrequent.

ARISTOTLE

To start with, we owe him the distinction between justice as the whole of virtue and justice as a particular virtue. In the former sense, being just is synonymous with being virtuous or moral. The religious notion of righteousness seems to be closer to this sense of justice. But, as a particular virtue, justice means fairness or equality: one is just in this sense if one does not take more than one's due. Aristotle's thinking about justice in this latter sense is a direct corollary of his more general theory about virtue itself, particularly of his doctrine of the 'golden mean'. Virtue, according to him, is the 'geometrical' mean between excess and privation, for example, courage, between foolhardiness and cowardice. Justice, likewise, is the mean between too much and too little. Just as there is an actual mid-point along the length of a given straight line which divides the line equally, so in principle justice can be located by pinpointing what is equal – that is, neither too much nor too little, neither the excess nor the privation of a given commodity or quality. Any allocation that is too much or too little is unjust because it is unequal. Another way of making the same point adopted by Aristotle is to say that justice is the neutral state (mid-point) between doing and suffering injustice. Here are Aristotle's own words:

> Just action is intermediate between doing injustice and suffering injustice, since the former is to get too much and the latter is to get too little. Justice is a sort of middle state, but not in the same manner as the other virtues are middle states; it is middle because it attaches to a middle amount, injustice being the quality of extremes. Also justice is the virtue which disposes the just man to resolve to act justly, and which leads him, when distributing things between himself and another, not to give himself a larger portion and his neighbour a smaller one of what is desirable, and the other way about in regard to what is detrimental, but to allot shares that are proportionately equal; and similarly when making a distribution between two other persons. . . . In an unjust distribution to get too little is to suffer injustice and to get too much is to do injustice.[1]

It should be clear that Aristotle is here referring, directly at any rate, to what he calls 'distributive' justice, which relates to the distribution of goods, such as money, honour etc., among people according to their desert. 'Corrective' justice, by contrast relates to rectifying injustices in transactions, for example, buying and selling, and so on, or those relating to crime and punishment. (This distinction has already been mentioned in the previous chapter. I bring it up here again in order to give an indication of its role in developing maxims or principles of justice.) Even in this regard, though, the judge can be said to be restoring fairness, equality or due proportion: he or she would be trying to determine if the price paid 'equals' the crime. One way or another, then, equality seems to be crucial to considerations of justice, and so is the need to keep irrelevant differences out. But there is no positive doctrine here about what are to count as relevant differences and what it is in respect of which equality is to be sought nor who are to be regarded as equals. It merely says 'give to equals equally', whatever it is that is to be given and whoever the equal recipients might be. It is important that the judge be impartial; and if a state administers its laws impartially through its judges, then the state can be said to be just.

'Political' justice 'exists between men living in a community for the purpose of satisfying their needs, men who are free and who enjoy either absolute or proportional equality. Between men who do not fulfil these conditions, no political justice exists, but only justice in a special sense and so called by analogy. Justice exists between those whose mutual relations are regulated by law; and the law exists for those between whom there is a possibility of injustice, the administration of the law being the discrimination of what is just and unjust.'[2] Aristotle is here making a distinction between 'political', and 'domestic' or 'private' justice. The justice of a father inside his family or of a master in relation to his slaves is to be contrasted with political or 'absolute' justice, which is 'regulated by law . . . and exists between persons naturally governed by law, who, . . . are people who have an equal share in governing and being governed'.[3] Children and slaves may be subject to domestic justice only, not political justice, for they are not equals, not being citizens of the state or community.

My primary interest here is in showing that in talking the way he does, particularly about distributive justice and political justice, Aristotle's thoughts provide the backdrop to some modern discussions of social justice. And much of the modern discussion tends to be about issues of social justice, even when the term ostensibly used is simply 'justice'. Modern theories of positive justice, that is, theories that advance claims as to what justice ought to be and why it is that we have to be just, can, as indicated earlier, be conveniently studied under three broad headings: (a) Liberal, (b) Libertarian, and (c) Socialist.

A liberal conception of justice attempts a synthesis, or compromise, between the respective demands of a libertarian (which takes liberty to be the ideal of justice) and a socialist conception (which regards equality to be that ideal). Consequently, a liberal tends to value both liberty and equality: more specifically, economic liberty and political equality. Understandably, its great appeal and its obvious shortcomings tend to arise from the difficulty of reconciling these two ideals. The liberal conception can be defended either by arguing that it is (or could be) the result of an actual or hypothetical agreement, or contract, freely entered into by rational agents; or else that this conception leads to the greatest happiness of the greatest number, and is, therefore, to be preferred for that reason. The former version can be called *contractual* liberalism and the latter *utilitarian*. In what follows immediately we will review some especially noteworthy examples of each tradition of philosophical thought.

CONTRACTUAL LIBERALISM: KANT

Although the 'social contract' theory is associated primarily with the names of such thinkers as Hobbes, Rousseau and Locke, Kant's exposition of the doctrine is widely regarded as a classic account of the blend of contract theory with the liberal ideas of justice and a wider conception of morality itself. According to Kant,

> Among all the contracts by which a large group of men unites to form a society . . . the contract establishing a *civil constitution* . . . is of an exceptional nature. For while, so far as its execution is concerned, it has much in common with all others that are likewise directed toward a chosen end to be pursued by joint effort, it is essentially different from all others in the principle of its constitution . . . In all social contracts, we find a union of many individuals for some common end which they all *share*. But a union as an end in itself which they all *ought to share* and which is thus an absolute and primary duty in all external relationships whatsoever among human beings (who cannot avoid mutually influencing one another), is only found in a society in so far as it constitutes a civil state, i.e., a commonwealth. . . .
>   The civil state, regarded purely as a lawful state, is based on the following *a priori* principles:
>   1. the *freedom* of every member of society as a *human being*
>   2. the *equality* of each with all the others as a *subject*
>   3. the *independence* of each member of a commonwealth as a *citizen*.
>   These principles are not so much laws given by an already established state, as laws by which a state can alone be established in accordance with pure rational principles of external human right.[4]

By 'freedom', Kant here means that every human being has the right to pursue his own happiness in whatever way he himself chooses, and not in accordance with what someone else may wish or decree to be good for everyone. It follows that if I wish to pursue my happiness free (or relatively free) from external constraint, everyone else must be deemed to be free in the same way. My pursuit of happiness has to be reconciled with that of everyone else under the framework of some workable general law. In a commonwealth of free individuals there is no 'paternalism': each human being is deemed to be capable of knowing where his happiness lies, and of pursuing the same in his own way.

The principle of 'equality' implies that each person has an equal right to coerce everyone else to bring his pursuit of happiness in consonance with everyone else's. 'All right consists solely in the restriction of the freedom of others, with the qualification that their freedom can co-exist with my freedom within the terms of a general law; and public right in a commonwealth is simply a state of affairs regulated by a real legislation which conforms to this principle and is backed up by power, and under which a whole people live as subjects in a lawful state.'⁵ In other words, in this commonwealth, the only constraint on anyone's freedom arises from the respect for the equal freedom of all subjects. It also implies the principle of equality of opportunity. In Kant's own words,

> From this idea of equality of men as subjects in a commonwealth, there emerges this further formula: every member of the commonwealth must be entitled to reach any degree of rank which a subject can earn through his talent, his industry and his good fortune. And his fellow subjects may not stand in his way by *hereditary* prerogatives or privileges of rank and thereby hold him and his descendants back indefinitely.⁶

The 'independence' of each citizen is, of course, presupposed by the social contract. 'An individual will cannot legislate for a commonwealth. For this requires freedom, equality and *unity* of the will of *all* the members. And the prerequisite for unity, since it necessitates a general vote (if freedom and equality are both present), is independence. The basic law, which can come only from the general, united will of the people, is called the *original contract*.'⁷

For John Locke this original contract is an actual one, but Kant regards it as only a hypothetical one. In fact, he thinks that the assumption that such a contract was actually entered into will require proof from history in the form of an instrument or some other record before we can feel bound by its provisions. Such a proof, however, is neither possible nor necessary. For Kant, therefore,

> It is in fact merely an *idea* of reason, which nonetheless, has undoubted practical reality; for it can oblige every legislator to frame his laws in such a way that they could have been produced by the united will of a whole nation, and to regard each subject, insofar as he can claim citizenship, as if he had consented within the general will.⁸

This approach to the social contract at the same time allows Kant to develop a criterion for the rightfulness of public legislation: a law is just only if the citizens of the commonwealth either would, or could, consent to it, if they considered it under conditions of impartiality.

Some of these Kantian ideas on justice are adopted, elaborated and systematized by John Rawls in his much acclaimed work, *A Theory of Justice*.

CONTRACTUAL LIBERALISM: JOHN RAWLS

> Thus we are to *imagine* (italics mine), [says Rawls], that those who
> engage in social cooperation choose together, in one joint act, the prin-
> ciples which are to assign basic rights and duties and to determine the
> division of social benefits. Men are to decide in advance how they are
> to regulate their claims against one another and what is to be the foun-
> dation charter of their society. Just as each person must decide by ra-
> tional reflection what constitutes his good – that is, the system of ends
> which is rational for him to pursue – so a group of persons must decide
> once and for all what is to count among them as just and unjust. The
> choice which rational men would make in this hypothetical situation of
> equal liberty, assuming for the present that this choice problem has a
> solution, determines the principles of justice.[9]

This statement provides the basis for Rawls' theory of justice as fairness.
This hypothetical choice situation is what he calls the 'original position'
of equality, which he regards as roughly corresponding to the 'state of
nature' in the traditional theory of the social contract. In order, however,
to ensure that people in this position would actually make the most rational
choices, unaffected by considerations of personal interest, Rawls stipulates
what he calls the 'veil of ignorance'. To quote him again,

> This original position is not, of course, thought of as an actual historical
> state of affairs, much less as a primitive condition of culture. It is
> understood as a purely hypothetical situation characterized so as to lead
> to a certain conception of justice. Among the essential features of this
> situation is that no one knows his place in society, his class position or
> social status, nor does anyone know his fortune in the distribution of
> natural assets and liabilities, his intelligence, strength, and the like. I
> shall even assume that the parties do not know their conceptions of the
> good or their special psychological propensities. The principles of justice
> are chosen behind a veil of ignorance. This ensures that no one is
> advantaged or disadvantaged in the choice of principles by the outcome
> of natural chance or the contingency of social circumstance.[10]

If these conditions are met, then, Rawls believes, people would actually
choose two rather different principles: 'the first requires equality in the
assignment of basic rights and duties, while the second holds that social
and economic inequalities, for example, inequalities of wealth and authority, are just only if they result in compensating benefits for everyone, and
in particular for the least advantaged members of society'.[11] This allows

Rawls to arrive at a 'Special Conception of Justice' as well as a 'General Conception of Justice.' He spells out the details of these in two different formulations – the second being more accurate and formal. The second formulation of these principles is as follows:

I. Special Conception of Justice
    1. Each person is to have an equal right to the most extensive total system of equal basic liberties compatible with a similar system of liberty for all.
    2. Social and economic inequalities are to be arranged so that they are both (a) to the greatest benefit of the least advantaged, consistent with the just savings principle, and (b) attached to offices and positions open to all under conditions of fair equality of opportunity.
II. General Conception of Justice
    All social goods – liberty and opportunity, income and wealth, and the bases of self-respect – are to be distributed equally unless an unequal distribution of any or all of these goods is to the advantage of the least favored.[12]

According to Rawls, the above principles will be chosen in the original position because people in this situation would find it reasonable to adopt a 'maximin strategy', that is, the strategy of maximizing the minimum pay-off for the least advantaged members of society. Since, given the veil of ignorance, no one knows whether he or she will turn out to be a member of the most, or of the least, advantaged section of society, it would be rational for each individual in the original position to ensure that the least advantaged member's share of the economic and political goods be as much as possible rather than as little as possible.

UTILITARIAN LIBERALISM: MILL

An alternative defence of the liberal theory of justice is provided by arguing that the requirements of justice are simply a sub-class of those that constitute the requirements of 'utility', that is, the greatest happiness of the greatest number, or the total happiness or satisfaction in society. The other terms used to refer to utility are sometimes 'public interest' or 'public utility'. The assumption made, as part of the utilitarian theory of morals, is that peoples' desire to seek happiness requires no defence or justification: it is what they naturally seek, and should do. And it is claimed, further, that the moral rules and principles that constitute the appropriate instruments of the total happiness of society happen, as a matter of fact, to include those that we regard as the principles of justice. Justice and utility are not separate, or even distinct, moral ideals: the former is only a part of the latter. Justice, therefore, receives its justification through being part of the moral, and natural, ideal of utility. Although there are many eminent philosophers, e.g. Bentham, Sidgwick, and Hume, whose names are associated with classical utilitarianism and the liberal theory of justice, the best known defence of the latter is generally considered to be Mill's.

In his *Utilitarianism*, he examines 'various modes of action and arrangements of human affairs which are classed, by universal or widely spread opinion, as just or unjust',[13] in order to find out what it is that constitutes justice and whether that is distinct from social or public utility. He argues that 'justice' seems to denote, in different circumstances, the idea of legal right, moral right, just desert, 'keeping faith', impartiality, equality or equal treatment, and conformity with either existing law or some 'ideal' law which does not yet exist but which ought to. After examining each of these separately and showing their connection with utility, Mill concludes that, 'Justice remains the appropriate name for certain social utilities which are vastly more important, and therefore more absolute and imperative, than any others are as a class (though not more so than others may be in particular cases); and which, therefore, ought to be, as well as naturally are, guarded by a sentiment, not only different in degree, but also in kind; distinguished from the milder feeling which attaches to the mere idea of promoting human pleasure or convenience at once by the more definite nature of its commands and by the sterner character of its sanctions.'[14] The so-called virtue of justice, according to Mill, is found, on examination, to be merely a sub-class of those qualities that are required to promote public utility. Its appearance of uniqueness is merely due to the 'sentiments' we come to attach to them in view of their importance for public utility or the happiness of society. The 'feeling of justice and injustice', according to Mill, is not *sui generis* like our sensations of colour and taste':[15] it is merely 'a derived feeling'. If human beings did not care about individual and collective happiness, justice would not have the aura of importance it seems to have.

Such in outline is the argument of other classical utilitarians also, in defence of the liberal view of justice. But utilitarianism, particularly its classical formulation, has been seen by many philosophers to have serious problems in accommodating justice. Indeed, it has been argued that justice and utility, at least in some circumstances, and, therefore, in principle, may be irreconcilable. For example, if maximum social utility is the goal, and if this can best be achieved by ignoring, or even suppressing, the interest of a minority, then the utilitarian must take recourse to such suppression. And yet we know that this will be unjust. Equally, it can be shown that the distribution of incomes in a society, for example, will be different depending on whether justice or utility is the criterion adopted: the latter may well allow greater inequalities than the former, which insists on fairness as against 'efficiency' or expediency. Contemporary utilitarians – R. M. Hare, among them – have offered various arguments which, they claim, adequately meet the objections to classical utilitarian defences of liberal justice. We are not now in a position to examine these arguments and counter-arguments. It should, however, be instructive to note that Rawls has no hesitation in rejecting the utilitarian justification of liberal justice. This does not mean that utilitarianism is finally and irrevocably out of consideration, or anything of that sort. But it does indicate how the best known contemporary contractarian views it.

LIBERTARIANISM: NOZICK

Whatever the difficulties in reconciling equality with individual liberty, there is no doubt that liberalism espouses individual liberty as an ideal of justice. Our summary of Kant's, Rawls' and Mill's views, above, should have made that clear. Not surprisingly, one of the classic defences of liberty as an ideal is Mill's pamphlet, *On Liberty*. In it he argues, forcefully and clearly, why individuals must enjoy the well-known freedoms: freedom of thought and expression, the freedom to pursue one's own happiness and the freedom of association. According to Mill,

> No society in which these liberties are not, on the whole, respected, is free, whatever may be its form of government; and none is completely free in which they do not exist absolute and unqualified. The only freedom which deserves the name, is that of pursuing our own good in our own way, so long as we do not attempt to deprive others of theirs, or impede their efforts to obtain it. Each is the proper guardian of his own health, whether bodily, or mental and spiritual. Mankind are greater gainers by suffering each other to live as seems good to themselves, than by compelling each to live as seems good to the rest.[16]

Libertarians are happy to accept this declaration from an illustrious liberal; but object that, within a utilitarian framework, the right to liberty cannot be primary, nor can it within contractarian liberalism: for in the former it must give way to public interest and in the latter to the demands of equality. For libertarians, liberty is the overriding ideal: it must not be sacrificed to any other. The liberal pursuit of utility or equality, seems to libertarians to allow for state manipulation or control of individual liberty. Libertarians, accordingly, formulate the principle of economic distribution quite differently. F. A. Hayek, for example, declares that the only equality that is compatible with the ideal of liberty is 'equality before the law'; and the only just principle of distribution is 'reward according to perceived value', and not 'reward according to merit'.[17] The libertarian frowns upon any suggestion of 'substantive' equality between men, and rejects any scheme designed to bring about this kind of equality. The 'market economy', operating according to the 'natural' laws of supply and demand, and free from state intervention, is the only economic system compatible with individual liberty. According to Milton Friedman, the principle governing the distribution of income in a free society is, 'to each according to what he or the instruments he owns produce'.[18] Besides, according to Friedman, the excess productivity that this system generates tends to give maximum benefits to society at large.

Robert Nozick, an influential contemporary libertarian, spells out this principle as 'from each as he chooses, to each as he is chosen'. This formula is a brief 'slogan' summarizing the larger statement of his principle which is as follows:

> From each according to what he chooses to do, to each according to what he makes for himself (perhaps with the contracted aid of others) and what others choose to do for him and choose to give him of what they've been given previously (under this maxim) and haven't yet expended or transferred.[19]

What a person can expend or transfer is determined by what he is justly 'entitled' to, and, therefore, the principles of justice are in effect equivalent to the principles of entitlement. There are certain principles of original appropriation, exchange and of 'rectification' (where the appropriation and exchange principles have been violated); and a person's holdings are just only if they meet these principles of entitlement. The principles of appropriation and exchange are subject, however, to a 'Lockean proviso',[20] which ensures that the acquisition and exchange is such that no one is thereby made worse off.

Nozick emphasizes that his 'entitlement principles' are different from the other principles of justice, for example, the liberal and socialist ones, in a very important respect. His principles are what he calls 'historical process principles', that is, they determine whether someone's holdings are just in terms of how these holdings originated. By contrast, according to Nozick, the liberal and socialist principles of justice are 'end-state principles' because they judge the justness or unjustness of holdings in terms of how they are, or are to be, distributed. What is, must be, wrong with end-state principles of justice is that they involve continual interference with people's lives; which, according to any libertarian, Nozick included, is against the ideal of individual liberty. In Nozick's words,

Whether it is done through taxation on wages or on wages over a certain amount, or through seizure of profits, or through there being a big *social pot* so that it's not clear what's coming from where and what's going where, patterned principles of distributive justice involve appropriating the actions of other persons. Seizing the results of someone's labor is equivalent to seizing hours from him and directing him to carry on various activities. . . . This process whereby they take this decision from you make them *a part owner* of you; it gives them a property right in you. Just as having such partial control and power of decision, by right, over an animal or inanimate object would be to have a property right in it.

End-state and most patterned principles of distributive justice institute (partial) ownership by others of people and their actions and labor. These principles involve a shift from the classical liberals' notion of self-ownership to a notion of (partial) property rights in *other* people.

Considerations such as these confront end-state and other patterned conceptions of justice with the question of whether the actions necessary to achieve the selected pattern don't themselves violate moral side constraints. Any view holding that there are moral side constraints on actions, that not all moral considerations can be built into end-states that are to be achieved . . . must face the possibility that some of its goals are not achievable by any morally permissible available means.[21]

This appeal to moral arguments in defence of a libertarian approach to justice tends, unfortunately, to do more than is strictly required of it. For it opens the door to rival moral arguments which claim that, equality as humans being a necessary condition of morality, the libertarian must be made to see that, in order for every individual to enjoy equality of respect and treatment, some existing economic and political inequalities have to be either removed or redressed, meaningfully. The moral implications of at least certain kinds of gross inequalities of power and wealth are so offensive that corrective action is *morally demanded*: what one should be (morally, as against merely legally, or by accident) entitled to, therefore, cannot be determined except by reference to some end-states.

SOCIALISM: MARX

The socialist conception of justice quite explicitly advocates what Nozick calls 'end-state principles'. Men are equal and so should have an equal share in the wealth, power and other goods of society; and only that political structure can be just in which people actually enjoy this right of equality of possession. If in order to bring about such a state of affairs, the deprived classes, the proletariat, or workers, have to take up arms to wrest power from the ruling classes, then such a revolution is inherently just and warranted. This revolutionary message is, of course, that of Karl Marx, but the doctrine that men are equal is, in a quite different setting, to be found in a dramatic statement by Hobbes:

> Nature hath made men so equal, in the faculties of the body, and mind; as that though there be found one man sometimes manifestly stronger in body, or of quicker mind than another; yet when all is reckoned together, the difference between man, and man, is not so considerable, as that one man can thereupon claim to himself any benefit, to which another may not pretend, as well as he. For as to the strength of the body, the weakest has strength enough to kill the strongest, either by secret machination, or by confederacy with others, that are in the same danger with himself.[22]

No doubt, a socialist principle of justice need not be based on the actual equality of people: the moral principle that they should be regarded as such, just because they are human, will be an adequate enough premise for socialism. Indeed, some will argue that moral equality is *the* basis. But, just assuming this 'original' equality to be a fact, how are people's actual inequalities of wealth and power to be explained? Marx's answer to the question is that the existing inequalities are the result of the exploitation of the many by the few, namely, the ruling classes. If work or labour, rather than capital, were to be regarded as the basis of the distribution of wealth, then each individual will be required to do work that he is best fitted to do and will in return receive goods proportional to his labour. The principle of justice in an egalitarian society will be: 'from each according to his ability, to each according to his contribution'.[23] Capital, or wealth, has accumulated in the hands of the few, because the principles of acquisition and exchange of holdings in traditional societies have been unjust, since they are unrelated to the value of labour in the productive process. According to Marxism, then,

The emancipation of labor demands the promotion of the instruments of labor to the common property of society, and the cooperative regulation of the total labor with equitable distribution of the proceeds of labor.[24]

This emancipation and the subsequent egalitarian order to be established require workers organizing themselves to acquire control of state machinery, as also taking certain other important steps. These steps are spelled out in detail in the *Communist Manifesto* (first published in English by Friedrich Engels in 1888), and list, among others, the following: abolition of property in land and application of all rents of land to public purposes; abolition of all right of inheritance; centralization of credit in the hands of the state; centralization of the means of communication and transport in the hands of the state; and free education for all children in public schools, and so on.[25]

It is evident that this degree of state control in bringing about a socialist order of justice into being seems quite contrary to the libertarian and liberal ideals of justice, primarily because it inevitably undermines individual liberty. Consequently, the Marxist ideal of justice, while helping to transform the world order, through its ideology and, especially the establishment of Marxist states in important parts of the world (until their disintegration in recent years) has at the same time tended to alienate 'free-thinking' individuals who prize the ideal of individual liberty. Democratic socialism claims to be able to achieve the non-exploitative socialist ideal of justice without the undue sacrifice of human freedoms, although it is conceded that the antisocial instincts of people have to be curbed. Equally importantly, democratic socialism shuns violent revolution as an instrument of social justice, and advocates gradual reform through progressive legislation. That a certain measure of socialism has found its way into the social legislation of modern democracies, is quite evident to any careful student of the scene.

But the advocacy, or adoption, of democratic socialism has not been the only answer of socialists to their critics who object to the loss of liberty and the preponderance of state authority. They argue that, even when such loss of liberty does occur, it ought, according to the teachings of Marx, to be regarded as a passing phase, marking the transition from 'bourgeois capitalist' to the 'proletarian' control of the instruments of power and production. When in due course, old 'exploitative' tendencies have been eradicated, and 'true' communism firmly established, there need no longer be any continuing loss of liberty or individual initiative; nor need there be any merely mechanical enforcing of equality of outcome:

In a higher phase of communist society, after the enslaving subordination of individuals under division of labor, and therewith also the antithesis between mental and physical labor, has vanished; after labor, from a mere means of life, has itself become the prime necessity of life; after the productive forces have also increased with the all-round development of the individual, and all the springs of cooperative wealth flow more abundantly – only then can the narrow horizon of bourgeois right be fully left behind and society inscribe on its banners: from each according to his ability, to each according to his needs![26]

The loss of liberty and the rule of collectivism, then, are merely necessary evils, to be endured while a truly cooperative, egalitarian, consciousness is being shaped in all of us. The two different slogans referred to above (the first on page 26 and the second at the end of the last quotation) are not seen by Marxists as being in mutual conflict: they represent principles of justice considered appropriate at different stages in the revolutionary process. When the dictatorship of the proletariat is first introduced, justice is served best by the first slogan. But when the communist utopia has been fully established – economically, politically and in respect of 'the all-round development of the individual' – then, in determining what an individual should be entitled to by way of economic and social goods, the appropriate principle of justice is no longer rights or deserts, but, simply need. And, of course, it is assumed that in such an ideal society there is no human need that cannot be satisfied!

3 The Idea of Justice in the Great Religions

In Chapter 2 we outlined what we had in Chapter 1 called rationalistic theories, especially its modern examples. Here we will try to discuss the other kind, namely, the metaphysical-religious conceptions of justice – not, indeed, all its examples, but only those illustrated by the great religions of the world. We start with Hinduism.

HINDUISM

Hindu conceptions of justice – whether in the sense of individual righteousness, or a moral and social order which it is our duty to preserve – seem to spring, directly or indirectly, from the *Rig Vedic* notion of *rta*, which denotes primarily the cosmic order, and, by implication, the order of the moral law, on the one hand, and the 'causal' order of the performance of sacrifices, on the other. Its centrality and importance in the *RigVeda*, the most ancient of the four Vedas, the 'revealed' literature of the Hindus, is clear and abundant. The gods themselves are born of the *rta*, and they follow the *rta*: they are practisers of *rta* and knowers of it.[1] Varuna, the chief god of the Hindu pantheon is its special guardian and truth its special expression. To be a follower of *rta* is to inculcate certain virtues: 'consideration in domestic relations, political loyalty, truth in friendships, abstention from crimes such as theft and murder and fidelity in marriage, especially demanded of women'.[2] In the *Brāhmaṇas*, the ritualistic portions of the Vedas, these moral virtues are indiscriminately interspersed with sacerdotal virtues – the importance of maintaining the purity of sacrifices and avoiding the 'sins' that follow from their improper performance.

In the *Smritis* and *Upaniṣads*, the historically later sections of sacred literature, this concept gives way to the cognate concept of *dharma* which stands for the cosmic order, the law, justice, morality and the very fabric of social order. One who follows *dharma* acquires merit by promoting the natural order. Although ritual and sacerdotal duties are still commanded as being one's *dharma*, moral and social virtues are emphasized too, especially in the *Grhya* and *Dharma sūtras*: truth, abstention from injury to the persons or properties of others, charity, hospitality, courage and devotion to duty and so on, being the main virtues.[3] Those failing to obey the dictates of *dharma* are threatened with punishment in the future life and the virtuous and just are promised rewards in like manner. The doctrine of *karma*, that is, that a man's place in life is determined by his deeds in a former life and that his moral or immoral actions in this life will determine his status and character in future lives, is seen as a corollary of the 'Natural Law', or *dharma*. Upholding *dharma* in all its manifestations – including, very importantly, the duties and obligations emanating from one's 'natural' place in society, that is, one's *varṇa* (caste) and *āśrama* (stage in life) – is upholding justice and social order. Transgressions are threatened with punishment not only in the form of a 'low' birth in another life, but also of a possible descent into hell, the kingdom of Yama. While upholding *dharma*, or the moral order, is extremely important, there is no doubt, however, that one's supreme end, *summum bonum*, is not *dharma*, but *mokṣa*, or liberation from the worldly cycle (*saṃsāra*), to be gained chiefly through 'knowledge' but also through devotion and 'action'. The practice of *dharma* itself can be a stepping-stone to *mokṣa*, the highest goal. In the *Upaniṣads* appears also the doctrine that all individual souls (*ātman*) are parts of one universal soul (*Brahman*), with which or into which they merge on liberation. This idea of *ātman* and *Brahman* provides at the same time the rationale, on the one hand, for the equal treatment of others – the corner-stone of justice – and, on the other, for the downgrading of earthly morality and justice, denying distinctions of any sort in the liberated stage.

While the Brahminical tradition continued to advocate the importance of the sacerdotal, ritual and esoteric aspects of *dharma*, the morality of popular Hindu culture found its expression in the epic literature, especially the two great epics, the *Rāmāyana* and the *Mahābhārata*. Not only precepts of personal righteousness but also the ideals of social and political action for the preservation of justice issued from these great books, as exemplified by the heroes of these popular stories. The most celebrated of these sources is the *Gītā*, which, although only a part of the *Mahābhārata* (and so not 'revealed' literature) still ranks among Hindus as a source of great authority and respect, especially on questions of justice and duty. Not only does it provide the philosophical ground for altruistic and compassionate action by emphasizing the unity of all being in *Īśvara* (God),[4] of whom Krishna is an incarnation; it also offers a deontological justification of social action, in a dramatic setting. Arjuna must fight his Kaurava cousins inspite of the killing of kith and kin involved, because as a *Kṣatriya* prince, it is his duty to fight for justice, whatever the consequences. Duty is to be done simply because it's duty and not because certain consequences might or might not follow from it. Personal inclination has no place in the context of the duty to restore justice (*dharma*). This exhortation to do battle because it is right to do so also enunciates, indirectly, the doctrine of a 'just war'. As if this personal exhortation were not enough, Krishna reinforces it with his exposition of the purpose of divine incarnation: God (personified here by Krishna himself) incarnates himself from age to age for the protection of the good, the destruction of the evil and the establishment of *dharma*, or justice.[5] That this *dharma* consists primarily in performing, in a non-attached way, the duties of one's caste and station in life, is not in doubt. But the fact is that *dharma* which represents personal duty is also at the same time the 'natural' order, the moral law, the repository of justice and virtue.

One other idea of particular significance in the context of justice that occurs in the epic group of literature is the notion of 'the golden age', the age of justice, peace and plenty. Any particular world, according to Hinduism, passes through various ages, epochs, or phases. It starts with *Trêtā*, the golden age, or the age of truth (*Satya Yuga*), but then, like any other construct, begins to decay and abound in evil and injustice, until at last, in the 'degenerate age' (*Kali Yuga*), it's only fit for destruction, to be followed by the 'recreation' of another world. The significance of this golden age idea is that it provides a source of ideals of justice – personal righteousness as well as social justice, not unlike the biblical idea of the kingdom of God. It was certainly a focal point in Mahatma Gandhi's formulation of a just social order: his adoption of the term *Rāma Rājya*, or the kingdom of Rama, while providing him with inspiration in spelling out his vision of a just social and political order, allowed him at the same time to harness popular support for his causes through the use of a popular but ancient concept. Gandhi, as well as some of the other modern social reformers of India, undoubtedly influenced by the active social ethic of Christianity, delved into the epics to fish out ideas and concepts that would allow them to counteract the distinctly other-worldly philosophy of renunciation that had become dominant in the Hinduism of India at the time. To Gandhi, at least, while the *Rāmāyana* provided the idea of *Rāma Rājya*, the kingdom of God, the *Gītā* furnished the basis of positive political action in the establishment of a just order and the removal of imperialism and injustice, as it did also for Tilak and certain other freedom-fighters and reformers.

BUDDHISM

Not surprisingly, Buddhism – at least early Buddhism – views righteousness as well as the idea of a just social order within the framework of the three Hindu concepts of *dharma*, *karma*, and *nirvāṇa*. As a non-theistic religion, it views righteousness as conformity, not with divine dictates, but with 'laws' of the natural order (*dharma*). Good actions which earn merit, therefore, are actions which are in keeping with this order: 'In the organic universe, right and wrong, and those consequences of actions which we call justice, retribution, compensation, are as truly and inevitably a part of the eternal natural or cosmic order as the flow of a river, the process of the seasons.'[6] The 'law' of *karma* is unyielding, so that right action always leads to reward and wrong action to punishment. But even the life of all possible rewards cannot be an ultimately desirable goal: that goal is *nirvāṇa*, or transcendence of the cycle of births and deaths. For existence is unavoidably tainted with pain (*duhkha*), the 'first noble truth' of the Buddha. Anyone who has assimilated the significance of the first 'noble truth', therefore, can only aim at the life of a saint (*arhat*): 'one who has become independent of the universe and free from any desire for it'.[7] This certainly remains the ideal of the Hīnayāna schools, the 'lesser vehicles', which emphasize that liberation can only be attained through personal effort.

In Hīnayāna writings, therefore, righteousness does not mean more than living according to the law. When a king, for example, is referred to as the virtuous king who ruled 'in righteousness' (*dhammena*) what is meant is that he lived according to his own principles of moral conduct.[8] Other terms used which have meanings similar to *dharma* are *śīla* and *charaṇa*. To become *śīlavata*, virtuous, is to follow the commandments, or *śīla*,[9] especially the 'five great' *śīlas*: truth, non-violence, non-appropriation, sexual continence and non-attachment. To grasp the first noble truth, and so, inevitably, to aim at the ideal of the *arhat* involves refraining from the ten 'fetters', including sensuality, ill-will, pride and arrogance.[10] The positive virtues to be cultivated are friendliness, compassion, sympathy and equanimity. But the cultivation of these negative and positive virtues is more a stepping-stone to the ideal of sainthood than the goal itself. The crucial part of the *arhat* ideal consists in getting rid of ignorance (*avidyā*) concerning the nature of things. Wisdom consists in realizing that compound things are painful, impermanent and soulless,[11] and given that, the truly desirable state can only be one of absolute independence from these things, desirelessness, remaining undefiled by contact with mundane things, and, positively, to become purified by wisdom.[12]

In Mahāyāna schools, the 'greater vehicles', while the ideal of the *arhat* is never explicitly abandoned, it seems to be gradually transcended by a superior ideal, that is, of becoming a *bodhisattva*. Everyone is potentially a Buddha, and by right resolve and action, but especially by the thought of enlightenment, one may, through numberless existences, eventually become Buddha. When one does become such a Buddha, *Tathāgata*, he may not only teach and inspire others by example: the merit that he has acquired in the process of becoming *Buddha* may be transferred to others. A *bodhisattva* is one who, '... has for numberless aeons practised the good conduct of well done *karma*, alms, morality, patience, fortitude, meditation, wisdom, resource, learning, conduct, vows and penance; he is endowed with great friendliness, compassion and sympathy; in his mind has arisen equanimity, and he strives for the weal and happiness of all beings'.[13] This idea of the *bodhisattva* has several profound consequences. In the first place, individual salvation need no longer be the individual's sole concern: the *bodhisattva* cares about and has compassion for all beings. Indeed, he comes back into the world to work for the liberation of all beings. Also, not just one's own merits, but even those earned by the *bodhisattva* may help one progress towards liberation. Sometimes, he is thought of as helping an individual to be reborn in *Sukhāvatī*, the Happy Land; and so devotion to him – *Amitābha* Buddha, or *Avalokiteśvara* – becomes desirable as a means to birth in the Land of Happiness, or *Sukhāvatī*. But perhaps the most fruitful idea to emerge from the concept of the *bodhisattva* – at least in the context of altruism and the creation of a just social order – is that of his compassion (*karuṇā*) for all beings: he will not forsake his fellow creatures. The larger justification for this attitude lies in the metaphysical doctrine of the non-existence of individual souls: all the selves are interlinked through the pool of *karmas*, past actions. The causal chain of actions and their consequences runs across individual body–mind complexes (*nāmarūpa*), and thus, in the long run, the liberation of one is the liberation of all. The *bodhisattvas* have compassion, because, in their wisdom they perceive the interconnectedness of things and beings, and the futility of the idea of individual liberation. In the *Vajracchedikā Sūtra*, this inseparability of the whole of being is expressed in the following words of the Buddha: 'All *bodhisattvas* should cultivate their minds to think: all sentient beings of whatever class are caused by me to attain the boundless liberation of *nirvāṇa*. Yet when vast, innumerable and immeasurable numbers of beings have thus been liberated, in truth no being has been liberated! Why is this Subhuti? It is because no *bodhisattva* who is truly so holds to the idea of an ego, a personality, a being or a separate individual.'[14] Hence the transformation of the *Buddha* into the *bodhisattva*, and the declaration of a community of beings, all sharing a common destiny and operating under a common causal nexus, the law of *karma*.

JUDAISM

Although there are many different terms used in the Old Testament to
denote justice, and other cognate concepts, probably the most frequent and
fundamental ones are *sedek, mishpat* and *ken*.[15] The first of these refers
rather more to righteousness and denotes what is true, right, fitting, or
conducive to the end in view; the second to judgment or justice and the
third means 'firm', 'free', 'fair', 'just', and so on. Being righteous con-
sisted, in one sense, in the practice of customary virtues, for example,
loyalty to friends, hospitality, generosity towards kindred, and the like.
But the righteous man is primarily 'the one who adheres loyally to the
moral and religious customs of his people',[16] while the wicked flout these
and threaten the fabric of society. The norms and principles of conduct
are, of course, to be found in the Torah which enshrines the covenant
between Yahweh and his chosen people, the Jews. The Torah, like any
other religious book of antiquity, contains maxims and precepts which are
a mixture of the moral, the ritual and the sacerdotal. These are supplemented
by the teachings of the prophets. Not unnaturally, the contents, emphases
and tones of the teachings of the prophets vary a great deal: from the lofty
ideals of justice found in Amos to the somewhat legalistic strains of Ezekiel.

All agree, however, that to be righteous is to do the will of God: for
God, Yahweh, 'exerciseth love, justice and righteousness in the world'.[17]
To follow the commandments of God is important not only because the
Jewish people have a covenant with God, and contracts must be obeyed;
but also because Yahweh is also a mighty God and a 'terrible' God and
punishes transgressors.

According to the *Encyclopedic Dictionary of Religion*, the three Hebrew
words, *sedakah* (justice), *hesed* (loyal devotion) and *salom* (peace) are so
closely interrelated that no one of them can be adequately explained without constant reference to the others.[18] The first of these, usually translated
'justice' in English, often has the force of 'genuine', 'true'. A person or
thing is *sedek* when he or it genuinely, or truly, is what he/it purports to
be. Hence the notions of 'just' or 'true' rain, and 'just' or 'true' weights.
Applied to human behaviour, this means that a man is just when he fulfils
his personal obligations arising from his membership of the family, the
community and other vows, commitments and covenants he has entered
into. Injustice consists in personal disloyalty, treachery, failing to fulfil
one's promises or one's other obligations. *Hesed*, or loyal devotion,
primarily signifies one's devotion to the covenant between God and the
Jews. God, the other partner in the covenant, never fails to abide by his
promises; and so it cannot be right for man to disobey his Law. Besides,

it is through each man doing God's will and obeying his commandments that a society secures peace and happiness for everyone, *shalom* or *salom*. What justice requires in terms of specific obligations can be spelt out in terms of laws to be obeyed. The Jewish concept of justice primarily signifies conformity with the Law, and only secondarily to norms and principles.

Understandably, a great deal of value is attached to the study of the scriptures in order to decipher what the Law is and then to loyally adhere to its dictates. Some prophets, however, are not content to see merely the letter of the Law being applied, but wish to give it a wider meaning and advocate grasping its spirit. With Amos, for example, 'righteousness is no mere body of customs', '. . . it is the living essence of social ethics, embracing alike honesty in business . . . and impartial justice in the law courts'.[19] While justice in the courts and in ordinary social attitudes tends generally to emphasize retribution, 'an eye for an eye and a tooth for a tooth', Hosea calls for mercy and love in the exercise of justice. 'As Jahweh has betrothed Israel to himself "in righteousness, justice, love and compassion", He expects them to be actuated by the same spirit towards one another.'[20] What he demands, above all, is love, *hesed*, brotherly love and kindness. Micah demands of all men 'respect for the three-fold principle of a righteous life – to do justice, and to delight in love, and to walk humbly with thy God'.[21]

While clearly, then, there is a lofty side to the interpretation of justice, especially in the greater prophets, by and large the framework of justice seems to be legalistic and retributive.[22] Adam and Eve's fall is the result of their sinfulness, and their sin lies in disobeying the command of God. The Old Testament God is very much a God of vengeance. The great flood, from which Noah saves himself and some other creatures, is the result of God's wrath, as are many of the diseases and disasters with which God threatens and punishes anyone found guilty of disobeying his commandments. The ruling motif seems to be punishment: Cain, Sodom and Gomorrah, Moses and Aaron have all suffered punishment at the hands of God. And in most cases the infringement they are guilty of is primarily disobedience of specific commandments or the entertaining or expression of doubt in God.

The Judaic idea of justice – in its individual as well as social aspects – was strongly intertwined with their experience of slavery in Egypt and their eventual liberation from this oppression under the leadership of Moses. For example, although slavery was not abolished by the Jews, being kind and considerate to the slave was encouraged. They are constantly reminded by Yahweh that they themselves were slaves at one time. Similarly, although the original idea of justice only involved being loyal and considerate to members of one's own clan, later on, hospitality and kindness to strangers as well was emphasized, on grounds that they themselves were strangers in Egypt once, and they must not treat strangers in the way they were treated.

More importantly, Jewish hopes of an ultimate national liberation gave rise to the belief in the coming of the Messiah and the kingdom of God to be established on this earth. This kingdom to be established was in a sense to be merely the restoration of what once already existed, namely, the kingdom of David, and the king was in fact to be a descendant of David. What is of significance for our purposes here, however, is that this kingdom was visualized to be the realm of perfect justice and happiness, a kind of second paradise.[23] The first paradise was lost through the fall of man at the beginning of this evil age, and would be restored again in the form of a Messianic paradise, which would last forever. In this kingdom, peace and prosperity will reign, people will be freed from pain and suffering, and death will no longer haunt human aspirations. In this 'garden of justice', '. . . the wolf will lodge with the lamb, and the leopard will lie down with the kid; the calf and the young lion will graze together, and a little child will lead them'.[24] The kingdom of God is, initially at any rate, viewed as a real kingdom to be established on earth in the near future under the rule of either Yahweh himself or the Messiah who will be a 'son of David', and is closely connected with the Day of Judgment. There are two somewhat different versions of events relating to the Day of Judgment itself. According to one, only the bodies of the just would be resurrected so that they could dwell forever in this new paradise: those of the unjust and the unrighteous will remain condemned to lie in the darkness of hell. According to the other, the bodies of all the dead would be resurrected; and the final Judgment would consist in the righteous being rewarded with eternal life in the kingdom of God, and the wicked being condemned to eternal torture in hell. Only later does the kingdom of God become a spiritual (rather than an earthly) and transcendental goal; and even then it barely does so in Judaism in any definitive fashion.[25]

CHRISTIANITY

Christian notions of righteousness and justice are, in one sense, merely the reiteration of Judaic ones, but in another sense, a revolutionary departure from them. This is not at all surprising: Jesus was, after all, a Jew; but quite unlike any other Jew that had ever lived before. Old Judaic ideas, therefore, receive startlingly new interpretations – or at least emphases. For example, although righteousness still consists in obeying the Law, the emphasis shifts from the Pharisaic cultivation of the letter of the law to cultivating the right condition of the heart. A mere adherence to the Law is no longer enough: the truly righteous person seeks to understand the real tenor of the Law which issues in right conduct. Not committing murder is important, but it is not enough: having murderous, or even angry, thoughts is contrary to the spirit of the Law. Refraining from adultery is important, but only because refraining from impure thoughts, itself, becomes the ideal. Prayer, fasting and almsgiving are still examples of right relationship with God and his creatures. Insofar as righteousness implies doing what is right, meaning 'according to the law', the teaching of Jesus transcends righteousness: it is, on the one hand, appealing to higher moral and spiritual principles; and, on the other, shifting the emphasis to being a particular kind of person, rather than merely obeying the Law. It is because the Pharisees and the Scribes are perceived by Jesus to be wedded to a narrow view of righteousness, that he mocks their ways and bids his disciples to do the 'real' will of God. His exhortation that the righteousness of his disciples must surpass that of the Pharisees and the Scribes,[26] certainly seems to imply that the mere mechanical, ostentatious following of the Law falls short of the true requirement of Law. It is possible to see this new emphasis as a return to the spirit of prophets such as Amos and Hosea, but, as a matter of fact, it is really a new departure, going well beyond what any of the prophets could have taught: Jesus transforms the old idea of righteousness to such a degree that it becomes arguable whether that concept has a central role in his teachings at all.

The transformation brought about by Jesus, however, is nowhere more dramatic than in the case of justice hitherto understood as retribution. His teaching is not to hate the enemy but to love him instead. The old rule of retribution, 'an eye for an eye and a tooth for a tooth', gives way to that of 'turning the other cheek'. 'Love thy neighbour' was not exactly a new saying, but never before until Jesus preached it had it enjoyed a central status in the social ethic. While this ideal of loving one's neighbour as oneself contains the seeds of a powerfully egalitarian doctrine of social justice, on the whole, it seems fair to say that justice is not the ruling concept in the teachings, or conduct, of Jesus: the very different ideal of love is taking its place. In a society truly governed by love, there is no need for justice; and Jesus' exhortation to his disciples is to be loving, kind, compassionate and forgiving. 'You have heard that they were told, "You must love your neighbour and hate your enemy". But I tell you, love your enemies and pray for your persecutors, so that you may show

yourselves true sons of your Father in heaven, for he makes his sun rise
on bad and good alike, and makes the rain fall on the upright and the
wrongdoers.'[27] If this is still justice, it is a highly sublimated form of
justice. I do not mean to imply that it is incompatible with love, for love
and justice are both qualities of God. But it would certainly seem to have
its sharp edges softened, making it difficult to render literalistic judgments
of what may or may not be just. This new 'justice', of love of God and
one's fellow creatures, irrespective of their deeds and characters, seems to
demand something different, at least something more, than the old justice
of simply punishing the wrongdoer, in accordance with laws. The law of
God thus becomes subject to two interpretations: the lower level, where it
is to be understood as obeying the existing laws and conventions; and the
higher, spiritual level, where it is to be understood as love, mercy, charity
and forgiveness. When it is appropriate to obey existing laws, when to
ignore, or oppose them, becomes a source of perplexity and ambiguity.
This ambiguity, moreover, characterizes Jesus' own answers to some of
the problems and issues raised, for example, on marriage and divorce,
family and other kinship ties, on paying taxes, and so on.[28]

A similar ambiguity seems to characterize Jesus' view on the kingdom
of God. He shares the prevailing Jewish belief that the-then world was
wicked and was coming to a close, to be followed by the kingdom of God.
The latter will establish a complete reversal of the existing order: 'many
who are first now will be last then, and the last will be first'. 'Blessed are
you who are poor, for the Kingdom of God is yours! Blessed are you who
are hungry now, for you will be satisfied. But alas for you who are rich,
for you have had your comfort! Alas for you who have plenty to eat now,
for you will be hungry!'[29] This talk of reversal, is at the very least, mys-
tifying. Is being poor a virtue which will be rewarded in the kingdom of
God, and being rich a vice to be punished? If so, it would seem that the
old idea of retribution is still hanging in the closet. If it is, on the other
hand, a way of indicating that material possessions are irrelevant as 'tickets'
to the kingdom of God, then why imply that in that kingdom, food or
clothing or other comforts could be sources of satisfaction, or happiness?
Is the kingdom of God to be understood as a material paradise, after all,
or as a new kind of spiritual realm where earthly possessions and cravings
will be redundant? The ambiguity also extends to questions about whether
this kingdom was physically to come into being or whether it merely
referred to an ideal to be worked for, irrespective of whether or not it was
actualizable. Furthermore, there are indications that Jesus thought that this
kingdom had already begun and was no longer merely a future possibility.
To say the least, the eschatological and the messianic visions of this kingdom

are hard to separate.[30] What does not seem to be ambiguous is that this kingdom will be the domain of love. And insofar as it will be a domain of justice as well, that is only because in God love *is* justice. He is the supreme judge, who on the Day of Judgment will decide who is or is not to be admitted to his kingdom. But if his justice is the same as love, why should there ever be a question as to who would enter the kingdom? Does not he love all – the rich and the poor, the good and the not-so-good, the righteous and the unrighteous? It is not that there are no answers to these questions. Quite the contrary, in fact. But what I earlier called the ambiguity of Jesus has allowed for very different, sometimes conflicting, answers even from theologians, not to mention ordinary believers.

ISLAM

It should be mentioned at the outset that Islam is a religion in the Biblical tradition which accepts many of the prophets of this tradition, including Jesus (although only as a prophet) – Mohammed, the founder of Islam, being another prophet and the source of a new revelation. The basic concepts and ideals of Islam in respect of righteousness and justice, as in many other respects, are akin to those of the older religions; although the emphases and orientation are uniquely determined by the personality of Mohammed and the sociopolitical climate of the Arab world. The two fundamental sources of guidance as to the moral and religious contents of righteousness and justice are: the *Korān*, the revealed literature, and the personal example of Mohammed, the *Sunnā*, the legal and conventional aide considered to be contained in the *Shariā*, the 'way' or the law. To be righteous is, above all, to have faith in God, *Allāh*, and to refrain from all thoughts of idolatry and polytheism of any sort. To be wavering in this respect is to be guilty of 'hypocrisy' which is the hallmark of unrighteousness. To be 'God-fearing', *muttaqi*, is a virtue which lies at the very root of personal righteousness. To associate with the unfaithful is hypocrisy as well, and, hence, the opposite of 'uprightness', *taqwā*.[31] 'O you who believe!', the *Korān* declares, 'Establish justice (*al-qist*), being witnesses for God – even if the evidence goes against yourselves or against your parents or kinsmen; and irrespective of whether the witness is rich or poor: under all circumstances God has priority for you (over your relatives)'.[32] Although God and his will thus unquestionably take precedence over all else, one's kinsmen are not to be shunned. In fact, the community (of believers) is a very important element in Islamic ethic; and hence the social virtues of charity, almsgiving and hospitality are extremely important too. The value of other 'good works' is recognized as well, but there is never any doubt left as to what comes first among virtues: complete submission to the will of God. '... whosoever submits his will to God, while being a good-doer, his wage is with his Lord, and no fear shall be on them, neither shall they sorrow'.[33]

The moral and religious goal of right conduct is thus laid down in the *Korān* and the *Sunnā*. But these do not provide specific details about the way in which these goals are to be achieved – not many, at any rate. The 'way' is to be found codified in the *Shariā*, which provides the framework for the establishment and administration of Islamic society. Since there were many different tribes in Arabia, frequently at odds with each other, *Shariā*, quite understandably, contains many different prescriptions, not always mutually compatible. But, be that as it may, it is this system of laws which governs Islamic practice in relation to social and legal affairs, such as marriage and divorce, taxation and the administration of justice in the law-courts. While it is wrong to attempt to simplify the contents of *Shariā*-law, it is perhaps not unfair to say that, on the whole, Islamic justice heralds a return to retribution as the principle of justice. In this respect, it is closer to the old Judaic practice than to its immediate predecessor among Biblical religions, namely, Christianity. It should be added, too, that while the divine authority of *Shariā* is not to be questioned, Islam recognizes that the interpretation of *Shariā* in concrete, evolving, situations, will involve an appeal to human reason, *ijtihād*,[34] by competent authority.

Finally, mention must be made of the idea of the kingdom of God in Islam – in a sense only a revival or reinstatement of the older Biblical idea, but especially prompted by the sociopolitical circumstances following the death of Mohammed. Although the first *Khalifā* (successor of Mohammed), Abu Bakr, was considered a very righteous man, *al-siddik*,[35] the 'righteous one', some of the later ones left much to be desired in this respect. Hence arose, or re-arose, the idea of Islamic messiah or saviour, *Mahdī*, who will come and deliver Islamic justice and the reign of righteousness. This belief is especially important in *Shiite* Islam, but is not rejected by the *Sunnis*. The *Mahdī*, it was believed, would be the twelfth *Imām*, 'whose name will also be Mohammed, whose patronymic will also be like that of the Apostle of God, and who will fill the earth with equity and justice, as it has been filled with injustice, oppression and tyranny'.[36] There is no dispute at all that when this kingdom arrives, the faithful will be resurrected and installed in this 'garden', especially if their deviations from righteousness have been minor. What will happen to the unfaithful, however, seems to be a matter of opinion: some believe that they will be condemned to eternal torment in hell; but others think that even they, after a period of punishment, may be allowed into the kingdom. There is some disagreement, too, as to whether the material rewards promised are to be taken literally or to be understood metaphorically only. There is hardly any dispute, however, that it is the will and judgment of God that will decide: the human individual has ultimately no say in what happens to his soul.

4 Social Justice and the Predicament of Religion

I hope the first three chapters have shown that the conceptions of justice, and their presuppositions, illustrated by rationalistic theories, especially their modern variants, are vastly different from those encountered in the great religions of the world. It should have become clear, too, that the notion of social justice, in its narrow sense, is very much a product of modern consciousness. While it is the centrepiece of liberal and socialist conceptions of justice – what Nozick calls 'end-state principles' of justice – it would be difficult to maintain that traditional religious conceptions of justice have anything much to do with it. The main concern of the latter is righteousness, the highest virtue to be displayed by individuals, both as a mark of character and as a determinant of social conduct. Justice, understood as righteousness, is, one might say, the whole of virtue, and not merely a particular virtue.

Given this sharp contrast between social justice, in its narrow sense, and justice as righteousness, one would have thought that it would be self-evident to everyone concerned that religion, properly understood, cannot be regarded as a tool of social justice. And yet this issue has been at the forefront of much recent theological debate. That this should be so is itself, perhaps, a tribute to the power of liberal and socialist thought. To what extent Vatican II itself was necessitated by this power may be hard to assess; although it would be equally hard to deny that it may have played a role. What seems certain, however, is that, especially after Vatican II, it was no longer so unusual to regard social justice as a legitimate concern of religion. This was because:

With Vatican II the Catholic church, as it were, turned itself inside out. Prior to the council Catholics were taught that their main business in life was to remain in the 'state of grace' and get to heaven. The church was the custodian of the means of grace and truth. In such a scheme earthly matters were ultimately inconsequential. At Vatican II, accepting and building on decades of work by theologians, the Catholic church modestly accepted its 'pilgrim' status, journeying alongside the rest of humankind. In a further radical shift the church began to see in 'human progress' evidence of God's working in human history.[1]

It should be added that the works of theologians to which reference has just been made were not necessarily all Catholics, nor, understandably, was the impact of Vatican II confined to Catholics. But, obviously, its influence on Catholics has been immense: so much so that even a fairly conservative pope, such as John Paul II, is apt to talk in the 'jargon of social justice'. For example, speaking to 'an enthusiastic group of priests and nuns' in Caracas, Venezuela, in 1985, the pope had this to say:[2]

There are sectors in which social progress and well-being manifest themselves in a luxurious egoism, while other sectors remain in poverty, on the fringes and illiterate. The church, committed to man, especially the most poor and alienated, cannot ignore these situations. It must not resign itself passively to leave these things as they are or, as often happens, to degenerate into worse situations.

There is a sense in which some at least of the pope's remarks may have been intended to 'upstage' Liberation theology in Latin America by showing that he and his church were equally concerned with questions of social justice. But it would be wrong to doubt his sincerity. Although, on the same occasion, he also directly tried to undermine Liberation theology by saying, 'To be faithful to the church is not to be taken in by doctrines or ideologies contrary to Catholic dogma, as certain groups of materialist inspiration or doubtful religious content would wish', what seems to me to be important is the expression of his belief that social justice is, and should legitimately be, the concern of religion – 'Catholic dogma' in this particular case. What his detailed prescriptions to the Latin American Catholic church were on how to go about achieving a more equitable distribution of wealth and power, I do not know. But it is clear that he wished the church not to resign itself passively to the existence of in-equalities and injustices in society. In other words, the church must become an instrument of social justice on earth – not only in Latin America, I would have thought, but everywhere else too. At a less grand level of hierarchy, let us take the very recent statement of a Roman Catholic priest who declared that: 'Social Justice is as important as worship. That is as religious as the prayers we offer in church.'[3]

Obviously, there are intermediate positions on commitment to social justice possible, which lie between the pope's – that of *not ignoring* situations of social inequity and that of the priest quoted above which regards commitment to social justice to be as important as worship or prayer; and they have been taken by various churches, or individuals among them. But they all seem to assume that social justice is an important goal of religion. I wish to challenge this assumption by arguing that it is a mistake to regard economic and political justice – which is what modern social justice is about – as a primary, or even significant, mission of religion. The temptation to think otherwise confronts religion with what I would like to call the 'predicament' of religion: namely, that traditional religion must regard 'spiritual salvation or liberation' as its primary objective, and can, therefore, only with difficulty, if at all, claim to be an instrument of economic or political liberation; non-traditional theologies, for example, Liberation theologies, on the other hand, while they can adopt political or economic liberation as their primary goal, must, in so doing, be compelled to make assumptions which are either theologically suspect or philosophically questionable, and potentially destructive of religion, by dragging it into the transient economic and political battles of the world.

Perhaps this predicament springs from another – a deeper and more historical one – which religion has had to face all along: namely, the need to accommodate the demands of earthly existence within, or alongside, religion's ultimate goal, namely the transcendental state of spiritual salvation or liberation, which must regard 'earthly matters' as 'ultimately inconsequential'. What I would like to maintain in this context is that any temptation to escape this predicament by reversing religion's priorities is just that; namely, a temptation, and, therefore, unwise. To make earthly concerns, such as social justice, the primary concern of religion, or even one on equal footing with spiritual salvation, while possibly securing some 'faithfuls' in the short run, is ultimately destructive of religion, by undermining its *raison d'être*.

I try to outline this case here, in this chapter, by raising some general questions which, singly and collectively, in my opinion, show why it is a mistake to regard religion as a tool of social justice. My claim is not that the two are incompatible. Far from it, in fact. Later in the book, I argue that religion may, indirectly, assist the cause of social justice; but only by pursuing its main mission of the spiritual and moral improvement of humankind, in a single-minded and dedicated way, and not by adopting popular earthly causes.

It may fairly be expected that I should outline here what I consider 'religion' to mean, especially since I have devoted some time to explaining what 'social justice' means. But there are two reasons why I will not here attempt to do so: firstly, because I have previously done so elsewhere;[4] and, secondly, because I have already introduced the conceptions of justice underlying the great religions of the world, which are far more easily recognized as specimens of religion than any definition claiming to show them to be so. In other words, I am here explaining the meaning of religion by pointing to instances of it that are already very familiar. In the case of the concept of social justice, however, I was not sure that everyone might already be familiar with it, in its narrow, technical sense.

Let me now, without further ado, come to the specific questions. My first question, very simply stated, is this:

(1) Since social justice is about the distribution of 'social goods' – liberty and opportunity, income and wealth, and so on; and religion is about turning our attention away from merely earthly concerns and towards a transcendent, other-worldly order of being and values, how can religion be regarded as being concerned with social justice, in any important way?

The reference above to 'social goods', and so on, is taken, it should be remembered, from Rawls' statement of the 'general conception of justice', outlined in Chapter 2: 'All social goods – liberty and opportunity, income and wealth, and the bases of self-respect – are to be distributed equally unless an unequal distribution of any or all of these goods is to the advantage of the least favored'. Justice here is about the equitable distribution of earthly goods, something religion cannot be said to be about, in any important sense, if at all. As another indicator of what social justice is really concerned with, let's look at another very influential liberal thinker, Bruce Ackerman, and his book, *Social Justice in the Liberal State*.[5] A glance at the table of contents, for example, shows what social justice is concerned with: the struggle for power, culture and right, wealth, citizenship, birthrights, liberal education, free exchange, trusteeship, exploitation, liberal democracy, and contract, utility and neutrality, and so on. If these are the concerns that social justice has come to encapsulate, then those who equate social justice with worship or prayer, and perhaps even those who regard it as an important goal of religion, must, it seems to me, have some other, looser, sense of social justice in mind; or else, they must – wittingly or unwittingly – be devaluing the transcendent goals and purposes of religion. If salvation, liberation, the complete, loving, submission to the will of God and the pursuit of righteousness and purity, and so on, are what religion is ultimately about, then it is difficult to see how it can take more than a cursory interest, if that, in social justice.

(2) Since the modern demand for social justice, as outlined by the liberal and socialist theories of justice, presupposes a 'secular humanist' framework of thinking, especially its optimistic assumption that we can 'fix' whatever is wrong with the world ourselves, isn't it the case that it challenges many of the important postulates of religious thinking: for example, human finitude and sinfulness; the limits to what human reason can unveil and our need to depend on God (or the other powers that might be), if we are to achieve anything at all?

The conflict between the rationalistic theories of justice – liberal and socialist in particular – and the metaphysical-religious ones – particularly those illustrated in the great religions – does not lie simply in the fact that the former are preoccupied with 'social goods' and the latter with 'spiritual goods'; although this conflict is important enough all by itself. It seems to go much deeper; liberal and socialist ideologies – with their insistence on social justice – arise out of the Enlightenment view of humans and their capacities, so often, and appropriately, dubbed 'secular humanism', especially by commentators on the religious right. This view implies that there is no ultimate reality higher than humans and no faculty superior to human reason. The world is for humans to do what they wish with it and in it; and their only help in working out their goals – their individual pursuits of happiness – is their reason. Reason dictates certain principles of justice, namely the principles of fair distribution of social goods. It seems to me evident that religion not only does not share some of these presuppositions: it must oppose them, if its own point of view is seen as deserving to survive, even as an alternative. It cannot forget about the finitude and sinfulness of human beings nor their greed and corruptibility. If human beings were indeed as self-sufficient as the Enlightenment credits them with being, then there would be no need for God or any other divine agency's help. Humans – with the aid of reason – could, then, achieve all they wished to, without any supernatural aid, prayer or worship. Anyone who thinks carefully about religion should be able to see that all this is completely contrary to the religious point of view: to think or speak in those ways is to be guilty of 'hubris'. And if religion must reject the postulates underlying the demand for social justice, then I would have thought that its concern with the latter could not be substantial or primary, if indeed it were appropriate at all.

Let me now raise my third question:

(3) It seems to me that the 'religious point of view' must see 'natural' inequalities and disadvantages as part of a supernatural or 'transcendental' design, and not simply as accidents of nature or history. The imperative of social justice, on the other hand, calls for corrective social action to remove or minimize these, because of the implicit assumption that these ought not to exist in any 'rational' social order. That these do actually exist is simply because of the workings of 'blind' nature or as unwanted vestiges of history. The seeking of justice is the attempt to impose reason – rational principles and goals – on what in itself would otherwise remain the domain of chance. But if religion is, almost by definition, precluded from regarding what is as the domain of mere chance, and must, instead, see it as part of some cosmic design or 'blueprint', then everything that

exists does so for some reason, even though we may not always be able to decipher what these reasons might be. If existing inequalities and disadvantages of individuals, however, are dictated by some 'divine', or other transcendental blueprint, then how can one be justified in removing them? The religious response would, I suppose, be that our duty to remove them, and, therefore, their actual disappearance eventually, may itself be part of the 'blueprint'. In other words, these disadvantages, when not due to 'man's inhumanity to man', could be seen as having been implanted on the natural order, so that we could, by our efforts, eliminate them, thus enabling us to become instruments in the execution of the transcendental design. This, of course, would be recognizable to many as one of the familiar lines of argument in some traditional theodicies. Now, whether or not this argument can be said to work in the context of a general theodicy, two things need to be said here in the specific context of justice. One is that if this approach is adopted, then, whatever the appearances, as a matter of fact, the inequalities and disadvantages of individuals will have to be seen as effects that ought not to be there ultimately, and, therefore, constitute, in the ultimate analysis, the realm of the irrational and the accidental. This implies arrogating to ourselves the ability to decipher what is supposedly the ultimate transcendental purpose, and so to declare some of it to be worth perpetrating and the rest fit only to be discarded. This may not only be questionable from the point of view of religious orthodoxy, but also indicative of less than total acceptance of the truly transcendental status of the 'blueprint'. At any rate, if in so choosing what part of the initial 'blueprint' is or is not worthy of retention, we have to rely on our own judgment, then it might well be simpler to disregard the religious need to read transcendental design in nature and society, and to accept human reason, by and in itself, to be the guide, and 'court of appeal'. Secondly, serious account must be taken of the fact that there is something morally very offensive about the thought that any deliberately designed transcendental 'blueprint' could actually apportion injustice to some individuals so that other individuals could learn to be just by trying to remove these injustices. Fairness dictates that no individuals be treated unjustly: and treating any of them as only a means, and not as an end, is acting contrary to the principles of justice, and, therefore, of morality; and even a divine agency may not alter this principle.

I now proceed to my fourth question:

(4) The modern notion of social justice considers individual rights and autonomy to constitute its core. We are autonomous in the sense that each one of us has the right to pursue our happiness in our own way, subject only to minor constraints, understood by the rationalistic theories in somewhat

different ways. No one else can tell me what is good for me: it's simply a question of what *I* choose to regard as my interests. As long as my pursuit of my chosen interests does not unduly interfere with those of others, I must not be interfered with. There are no external authorities to whom I am obliged to listen. I obey the 'just' laws of my state, only insofar as I regard myself as a party to the institutional arrangements, called state, society, and so on. It needs no explaining how antithetical all this is to the religious way of thinking. According to the latter, my will must be subservient to the will of God, or other divine powers. My rights, if any, in this world cannot be those of ownership, but only those that we can be said to enjoy as if we were guests or borrowers in the world. I cannot be free to pursue whatever I choose as my happiness. For there is a right and a wrong, a noble and an ignoble pursuit; determined not by me, but the higher powers or agencies. I must do what is right – the will of God, or *dharma*, or whatever – and not be preoccupied with my rights and interests. If I have problems determining what is right, either generally or on a specific occasion, I must listen to the scripture, the priest and the holy man for guidance. 'Thy will be done!', is a very different attitude from, 'My rights must not be trifled with!'. None of this implies that the religious person, acting out of his sense of charity, love or compassion, should not do 'good works' that result in the alleviation of human suffering – whether it is from poverty, disease or oppression by a thoughtless dictator – but the language of 'rights' and 'justice' is a fundamentally different one from that of 'charity', 'love', or 'compassion'. The question that I wish to end with here is this: How can religion simply adopt social justice as its primary goal, without accepting the baggage of suppositions the notion carries, and which happen to be diametrically opposed to the religious way of thinking?

My fifth question is as follows:

(5) Since the demand for social justice frequently involves emancipation from the tyrannies of history and historical institutions; and since religion itself may, in many circumstances, be justifiably viewed as a source or instrument of such tyranny, how can religion serve at the same time as an oppressor as well as a liberator? It does not need arguing that traditional religion has been a conservative force, used to justify and buttress institutions and practices from many of which we seek emancipation in the name of justice. Traditional religious doctrines and dogmas have been used to support slavery, the divine right of kings to rule and of men to keep women in subjugation. The desire to perpetrate these injustices probably came from the natural urge to preserve one's own privileges; but it was religion which freely provided the doctrinal and institutional support

for them, in each case, by creating appropriate myths and models. Consequently, justice in these cases has meant liberation from the accompanying false religious myths, models and dogmas, at least as much as from the actual acts of injustice themselves. It would take a lot of sophistry, I think, to deny that women's inferior status in society owes a great deal to traditional religious myths about woman being mere 'nature' and passive, and man representing the realm of culture, reason and creativity.[6] On a more down-to-earth note, can anyone envision justice in Northern Ireland without the subversion of the role of religion there; or peace in the Middle East, without 'secular reason' replacing religious intolerance? In these instances, at least historically, religion is the very source and instrument of prevailing injustices and unrest; and there would seem to be no way of securing justice for all concerned, except by transcending, or transforming religion altogether.

It may, quite rightly, be said that these examples represent the deliberate and misguided misuse of religion for political purposes; and so they provide no genuine basis for my case against religion itself. There may be more than a grain of truth in this assertion. For my point is not, and cannot be, that there is anything in the concept of religion itself which would make it a tool of injustice. What I am arguing is simply that social justice, *as a matter of fact*, frequently demands release from the tyrannies of tradition itself; and traditional religion is so important a part of this tradition, that it may be impossible to reach the goal of justice without debunking relevant religious dogmas and practices. And to the extent that this is so, it may be more than odd to think that at least traditional religion can be an instrument of social justice.

(6) The last question discussed brought out not a conceptual but a historical or practical problem involved in regarding religion as an appropriate tool of social justice. My final, and sixth question, is of a similar sort, but oriented more towards the future than the past. It seems to me that the heavy involvement of religion in issues of social justice inevitably draws religion deeply into politics and, therefore, possibly into political quagmires. Some examples of those were offered above, and many more can no doubt be drawn from history. The question that needs to be asked is this: Should not religion, learning from past mistakes, avoid undue involvement in issues that drag it more and more deeply into the realm of politics, and thus make it possible, even likely, that its religious mission – namely, its primary concern with the spiritual and moral uplifting of humans – could be compromised, diluted or even abandoned?

The problems in refraining from such involvement may be twofold. The first is the practical difficulty – considerable, indeed – in actually keeping religion and politics apart, even where this principle has been conceded. This will be discussed further in Chapter 8. The other difficulty is of a different kind. Sometimes political involvement may seem to pay dividends to religion, by temporarily drawing more attention to itself from those whose political cause is being championed; and thereby help to swell the number of adherents. But I am not convinced that this gain is worth the price that religion pays over the long run, or even immediately. It does not have to be argued that for every party or group whose political interests religion undertakes to champion at a given time, there is always another which feels betrayed. And this frequently will come to haunt religion, allowing doubts to be raised about its true commitments – namely, its spiritual and moral mission. It also creates distrust and hatred in the opposition camp, thus sowing the seeds of future divisions, vendettas and injustices. And finally, but not unimportantly, any heavy involvement of religion in merely mundane matters – whatever the short-term gains – ends up discrediting religion as being more concerned with material than spiritual matters. What may seem, initially, to draw extra members to the church, may end up, in the long run, in people's failure to see religion as an institution with a focus on things far removed from those that seem to concern most of us most of the time, and thus as unique and commanding respect.

I conclude this chapter by emphasizing that, while religion, in my opinion, is not, and should not be seen as, the tool of social justice, in the narrow sense of the phrase we have been exploring, I do not mean to imply that religion can, or should, be indifferent to questions of justice altogether. It may – in fact, it must – quite appropriately, preach and propagate the very different vision of a just social order, as encapsulated in the idea of the kingdom of God. As I try to show in Chapters 10 and 11, this idea, contrary to appearances, is not about economic and political well-being; but about the spiritual and moral transformation of human beings in keeping with their ultimate destiny. It is, therefore, very much the concern of religion.

I maintain also that even in the context of social justice in its narrow, specialized sense, religion may have an indirect, but beneficial, role to play, insofar as it succeeds in instilling moral values in humans and in weaning them away from mere material concerns, thus curbing their tendency towards heedless consumerism, selfishness and greed. Finally, personal righteousness is very much the concern of religion; and it can be argued that a society in which righteousness prevails, would tend to have less injustice, even of the economic and political kind. But there will be more discussion on the indirect role of religion in social justice in Chapter 6.

5 Liberation Theology and Social Justice

As we saw in Chapter 3, traditional religion does not have a great deal to say on social justice, for this conception of justice is very much a product of modern consciousness; and in Chapter 4 we outlined some of the problems involved in regarding social justice as a primary concern of religion. This is not to say that certain traditional religious concepts, episodes and symbolism cannot be interpreted in ways that would seem to have a very explicit message on issues that are considered central to this narrower conception of social justice. Indeed, it is because such reinterpretation has been found to be possible that modern social reformers, of a religious persuasion, have considered it fitting to spread their 'gospel' of change, without having to abandon their religious framework. And such reformers have arisen within practically all the major faiths, and right round the world. In Latin America, however, there has been a significant contemporary movement claiming that, insofar as traditional Christianity has failed to see this kind of social justice as its primary goal, it has missed the point of original Christianity and of the person and message of Jesus Christ. This movement, particularly the theology behind it, is known as Liberation Theology; and is the subject of our discussion in this chapter.

According to these Latin American thinkers, the chief message and preoccupation of original Christianity, that is, of first century AD Christianity, was the economic and political liberation of the poor, the oppressed and the weak in society. It was, according to them, the European influence, especially that of Greek ideas, that made the original church see spiritual liberation as its primary preoccupation. Christianity, especially Catholicism, must return to the original message of economic and political liberation for the masses; and the church must become an active force in the struggle for such liberation. There are many different Latin American thinkers who preach this message (and, following their example, similar efforts have been made by Asian, African-American and feminist thinkers, outside Latin America). Understandably, not all of them agree on every detail, nor in their overall political orientation. But it has become customary by now to call the thoughts of these people 'Liberation Theology', or the 'Theology of Liberation'. The chief Liberation theologians among Latin Americans are Paulo Freire, Gustavo Gutierrez, Juan Luis Segundo, Leonardo Boff and Hugo Assman.

It may be useful to add here that three factors have played particularly important roles in this 'politicization' of Christianity witnessed in Liberation theology. Foremost among them was the perception of ever-increasing poverty and indebtedness among the peoples of the Third World alongside the increasing affluence of the industrialized democracies; and the failure of the latter to pay anything but lip-service towards the establishment of social justice in the poor countries of the world, including those in Latin America. An important part of this perception involved the phenomenon of oppressive military dictatorships, usually aided and abetted by the rich democracies, for their own purposes. This perception had led to a disillusionment with the pious-sounding, but ineffective, declarations of goodwill of the democracies, and more generally with the power of democratic methods to bring about the required changes. An important fillip to the struggle for social justice, within the framework of the Catholic church, was provided by the Second Vatican Council which, as pointed out in the last chapter, encouraged the church's involvement in social issues. But, almost certainly, the most important factor has been the influence of Marxism, and its message of socialism and class struggle. The success of Cuba in raising the living standards of its masses clearly had a salutary effect. But while all Liberation theologians would almost certainly be happy to be called 'socialists', their commitments to Marxism and its methods vary a great deal. Hugo Assman is, arguably, the most outspokenly Marxist among them.

Whatever the differences among Liberation theologians in respect of loyalty to specific ideologies, and in other respects, certain basic themes seem to be common. There is hardly any disagreement among them that what they call 'Western' theology has been narrow in scope, primarily because of its excessive preoccupation with right belief, rather than authentic practice, *praxis*. They advocate a fundamental reorientation of the theological axis towards the political dimensions of liberation-oppression. This in turn requires a thorough critique and new understanding of the important traditional theological concepts, for example, faith, love, salvation, sin, freedom and so on. The following passage from Gutierrez can be used to set the scene for the programme of re-evaluation:

> In the past, concern for social praxis in theological thought did not sufficiently take into account the political dimension. In Christian circles there was – and continues to be – difficulty in perceiving the originality and specificity of the political sphere. Stress was placed on private life and on the cultivation of private values; things political were relegated to a lower plane, to the elusive and undemanding area of a

misunderstood 'common good'. At most, this viewpoint provided a basis for 'social pastoral planning', grounded on the 'social emotion' which every self-respecting Christian ought to experience. Hence there developed the complacency with a very general and 'humanizing' vision of reality, to the detriment of a scientific and structural knowledge of socioeconomic mechanisms and historical dynamics. Hence also there came the insistence on the personal and conciliatory aspects of the gospel message rather than on its political and conflictual dimensions. We must take a new look at Christian life; we must see how these emphases in the past have conditioned and challenged the historical presence of the Church. This presence has an inescapable political dimension. It has always been so, but because of new circumstances it is more urgent that we come to terms with it. Indeed, there is a greater awareness of it, even among Christians. It is impossible to think or to live in the church without taking into account this political dimension.[1]

Christian faith, according to Liberation theologians, must cease to be merely a preoccupation with private virtues; and it must no longer relegate social and political practice to the demands of the supposedly higher spiritual concerns. They argue that this sort of bifurcation between private and public virtues and spiritual and earthly concerns is foreign to the spirit of the Bible, and owes its origins to the 'Europeanization' of the gospel message in the post-Constantinian church. Traditional Western theology has understood its task to be, primarily, the systematization of transcendent truths which correspond with the realities of a transcendental realm. Faith, accordingly, has been understood as the acquisition of these truths and, therefore, regarded as a certain state of belief. The emphasis, consequently, has been on right belief, and not, as it should have been, on right action, or *praxis*. This fundamental dualism between the transcendent and the earthly, the spiritual and the bodily, the intellectual and the practical and between private virtue and social-political duty, springs from the Greek influence on the early Christian church, and is not consistent with the earlier Biblical tradition. The Old Testament does not separate the mortal body from the immortal soul, and has not much time for the dualistic train of thought which dominates Western theology. It is the influence of Plato and Neo-Platonism that makes Christianity adopt a dualistic ontology. It is this dualism that makes Augustine split the universe into the City of Man and the City of God – a split which seldom leaves Christian thinking down the centuries. Man's highest concern has, quite understandably, been supposed to be this higher realm of spiritual truths, and faith has been seen as the acquisition and assimilation of these. This rendering of faith as something private and cognitive has distorted the proper perspective. This need not, however, remain the case if knowledge is understood in true Biblical fashion. In the Bible, knowledge is regarded as the basis of practical activity, and not as a peep into transcendence. As it is the basis of practice, its vindication does not lie in abstract theological speculation but in the way it informs and shapes our lives.

And the same goes for faith. According to Bonino, another Liberation theologian:

> Faith is always a concrete obedience which relies on God's promise and is vindicated in the act of obedience: Abraham offering his only son, Moses stepping into the Red Sea. . . . [T]he faith of Israel is consistently portrayed, not as a *gnosis*, but as a *way*, a particular way of acting.[2]

According to Gutierrez, 'Faith reveals to us the deep meaning of the history which we fashion with our own hands: it teaches us that every human act which is oriented towards the construction of a more just society has value in terms of communion with God – in terms of salvation; inversely it teaches that all injustice is a breach with him.'[3]

As Liberation theologians see it, traditional Christian theology has also misconstrued salvation as consisting merely in the salvation of the soul or spirit. But there is no separation between spiritual and temporal salvation in the Bible. Jesus was as much concerned with physical as spiritual needs. He not only taught the love of God, but also the love of man; and his ministry was as much about healing the sick and restoring sight to the blind, as it was about a proper relationship between man and God. This sundering of the two elements of salvation is, once again, a legacy of Western dualism implanted on Christian thought. Positively un-Biblical, however, is the emphasis on personal purity and good intentions as the means to salvation. Although *merit* is recognized as a condition for salvation in Catholic theology, it is understood as referring primarily to intentions rather than to the desirable consequences one might be able to bring about. As Segundo puts it:

> The fact is that in the Catholic view the merit of a human action had no direct relationship to its historical effectiveness. Neither successful endeavors nor unsuccessful endeavors are meritorious *as such*. The historical end result of human actions, in other words, does not have anything directly to do with totalling up a person's merit. What really counts is the effort expended and a God-directed intention. To use a doctor as our example here, the current conception of merit is not concerned at all with whether the patient is cured or not. What gains merit

for the doctor is the effort he makes to cure the patient and the intention to do that for the glory of God rather than for the sake of fame or the life of the patient. The latter merely serves as the occasion for merit.[4]

This view could only have been found acceptable on the supposition that the result of actions in this world had ultimately no significance in the context of the supernatural goal of final salvation. Consequently, it was considered appropriate for the church to be an interested observer, or at best, involved critic, of historical and political institutions, but not to be an active instrument of change. All Liberation theologians agree that salvation primarily involves liberating the masses from its poverty, and oppression under unjust regimes: salvation is not release from the world, but a transformation of the world economic and political order. And it certainly is not a private affair, each seeking his/her own salvation: salvation is a collective goal and the road to it is social cooperation and class struggle.

This new understanding of salvation also transforms the view of *sin* taken. According to Gutierrez,

. . . in the liberation approach sin is not considered as an individual, private, or merely interior reality – asserted just enough to necessitate a 'spiritual' redemption which does not challenge the order in which we live. Sin is regarded as a social, historical fact, the absence of brotherhood and love in relationships among men, the breach of friendship with God and with other men, and, therefore, an interior, personal fracture. When it is considered in this way, the collective dimensions of sin are rediscovered. . . . Moreover, sin does not appear as an afterthought, something which one has to mention so as not to stray from tradition or leave oneself open to attack. Nor is this a matter of escape into a fleshless spiritualism. Sin is evident in oppressive structures, in the exploitation of man by man, in the domination and slavery of peoples, races, and social classes. Sin appears, therefore, as the fundamental alienation, the root of a situation of injustice and exploitation. . . . Sin demands a radical liberation, which in turn necessarily implies a political liberation . . .[5]

This way of understanding sin paves the way to the solidarity of the oppressed directed towards overcoming all that stands in the way of man's freedom. As Ignacio Ellacuria puts it,

We must get beyond the partial notion of sin as a merely individual violation of some law. We must recover the social dimension of sin as the annulment of God's presence among human beings and the domination of evil which prohibits the freedom of God's children.[6]

This 'social dimension' of sin is encountered wherever injustice and oppression exist; and a failure to take steps to eradicate these involves living in a state of sin. To be converted to the cause of removing social injustice is the true spiritual conversion, which according to Liberation theologians, is not 'an inward-looking private attitude, but a process which occurs in the socioeconomic, political and cultural medium in which life goes on, and which is to be transformed'.[7] 'To be converted is to commit oneself to the process of the liberation of the poor and oppressed, to commit oneself lucidly, realistically and concretely. It means to commit oneself not only generously, but also with an analysis of the situation and a strategy of action.'[8]

The same message of social involvement and deep commitment to eradicate social injustice, wherever it is found, is entailed, according to Liberation theologians, in the idea of Christian love, properly understood. According to Gutierrez,

> The universality of Christian love is only an abstraction unless it becomes concrete history, process, conflict; it is arrived at only through particularity. To love all men does not mean avoiding confrontations; it does not mean preserving a fictitious harmony. Universal love is that which in solidarity with the oppressed seeks also to liberate the oppressors from their own power, from their ambition, and from their selfishness. . . . One loves the oppressors by liberating them from their inhuman condition as oppressors, by liberating them from themselves. But this cannot be achieved except by resolutely opting for the oppressed, that is, by combatting the oppressive class.[9]

Not only, then, is class struggle consistent with Christian love, and not only does active class struggle express love for the oppressed: to oppose the oppressor class is also an act of love toward the oppressor. Not to show love, in action, of this kind is failing to do the Christian duty of loving God. Universal love, as we have just seen, entails, according to Liberation theologians, not just showing solidarity with the oppressed classes but also, systematically subverting the institutions created by the oppressor class.

It is this teaching of subversion of the *status quo* and of engaging in a class struggle, especially if it involves recourse to violence, that is seen by traditional Christians to be the most objectionable feature of Liberation theology. And it is not just that violence, revolutionary or otherwise, is morally wrong: it is seen to be especially wrong for a Christian. Did not Jesus, after all, preach the doctrine of turning the other cheek and loving the enemy? Isn't this the most distinctive feature of Christianity? And if so, then the recourse to violence must be a positively un-Christian act?

Liberation theologians take the view that such an understanding of the Christian message, traditional though it is, is somewhat simple. For it seems to be based on an over-emphasis on certain isolated passages in the Bible,[10] and on only some episodes in the life of Jesus. Although Jesus did not preach the overthrow of the Roman empire, nor explicitly advocate the subversion of the existing order, there is enough ambiguity in his teachings to allow the interpretation that such indeed was his message. At any rate, there is no doubt that he was perceived as an enemy of the established order. Otherwise, he would not have been crucified. Liberation theologians emphasize that the message of Jesus is complex and far-reaching, and should not be read in a simplistic way. 'The liberation which Jesus offers is universal and integral; it transcends national boundaries, attacks the foundation of injustice and exploitation, and eliminates political religious confusions, without therefore being limited to a purely "spiritual" plane.'[11] Eloquent and ingenious though this defence of revolutionary violence might be, there is no question that it remains highly controversial as an authentic interpretation of the message and person of Jesus Christ.

The foregoing should have made it clear that Liberation theologians take a different view of theology itself. According to them, theology is not an abstract, neutral discipline which merely provides a rational systematization of truths and doctrines about the transcendent. It has to do with deeds rather than words: its primary concern is *praxis.* According to Gutierrez, again, theology is a critical reflection on *praxis*, which emphasizes the 'existential and active aspects of the Christian Life'. 'In the first place', according to him,

[C]harity has been fruitfully rediscovered as the center of the Christian life. This has led to a more Biblical view of the faith as an act of trust, a going out of one's self, a commitment to God and neighbor, a relationship to others. . . . According to the Bible, faith is the total response of man to God, who saves through love. In this light, the understanding of the faith appears as the understanding not of the simple affirmation – almost memorization – of truths, but of a commitment, an overall attitude, a particular posture toward life.[12]

In this view, theology ceases to be merely the learned 'dispensations' by, and disputations among, theologians; it becomes an active tool for social justice, reform and, if necessary, revolution. The title, *Liberation of Theology*, of Segundo's book, cited earlier, is not accidental: it is meant to proclaim the radical reinterpretation of theology intended by Liberation theologians.

This is a bare outline of Liberation theology: and that, too, only of its theological tenets. It does not even pretend to capture the non-theological aspects of what was – perhaps still is – a revolutionary movement, with reasonably wide support even among clergy, its 'base communities', its programme of raising the consciousness of the oppressed masses, *concientizacion*, its popular appeal or the repression it suffered under tyrannical military regimes and the martyrs that it produced, such as Camilo Terres.[13] Those in Latin America, and elsewhere, who are committed to ending poverty, corruption and oppression in certain parts of the world, find in it a powerful voice and an ideology of change within a religious framework. But others see in it doubtful scholarship, inauthentic history or a distortion of true religion and theology, if not all of these at the same time. The transforming of theology into ideology – Marxist ideology, in particular – becomes the specific target of some critics; while others even dismiss it as a mere 'fad'. Not unexpectedly, the most sustained opposition to Liberation theology has come from the Catholic church, which has included reprimands of figures such as Gutierrez and Leonardo Boff, not to mention public and official criticisms of the message and methods of Liberation theology. The most famous of these critiques is the so-called 'Ratzinger letter' ('Instruction on Certain Aspects of the Theology of Liberation', issued in August 1984, by Cardinal Joseph Ratzinger, the head of the Vatican's Sacred Congregation for the Doctrine of the Faith) which was sent in 1983 to Peruvian Bishops and which listed the objections to the theology of Gustavo Gutierrez. This 'letter' 'repeatedly accuses liberation theology of a "reduction" that ignores basic elements of Christianity: of reducing sin to social structures, of making the struggle for justice the whole essence of salvation, of reducing the gospel to a purely earthly gospel, of equating truth with partisan praxis, of denying "the transcendent character of the distinction between good and evil . . ."'.[14]

As the last paragraph indicates, Cardinal Ratzinger takes issue with Liberation theology on many counts. I want to pick out for particular attention two of these, as samples. The first of these, while not discouraging church people from striving for human rights, warns against the use of revolutionary violence in this battle, which, Cardinal Ratzinger says:

> must be fought in ways consistent with human dignity. That is why the systematic and deliberate recourse to blind violence, no matter from which side it comes, must be condemned. To put one's trust in violent means in the hope of restoring more justice is to become the victim of a fatal illusion: violence begets violence and degrades man. It mocks the dignity of man in the person of the victims, and it debases that same dignity among those who practice it.[15]

I am sure that Mahatma Gandhi, the great fighter for social justice, would have whole-heartedly supported the sentiments expressed here. We have seen that Liberation theology does advocate the use of violence in the revolutionary class struggle it preaches.

The other point that I wish to refer to is also especially interesting, coming as it does from a luminary of the Catholic church, with a history of involvement in politics. Ratzinger says: 'One needs to be on guard against the politicization of existence which, misunderstanding the entire meaning of the kingdom of God and the transcendence of the person, begins to sacralize politics and betray the religion of the people in favour of the projects of the revolution.'[16] Whatever the irony involved in this observation, it does, in my opinion, make a good point in favour of the separation of religion and politics, a theme I have more to say about in Chapter 8. For the moment, all I wish to urge here is that if religion is seen as merely an instrument of political and economic liberation, of social change, of the reversal of the status quo, where does its distinctiveness lie? In what respect is it different from politics or ideology?

My reasons for citing the Ratzinger letter so importantly here are twofold: first, I am not an expert on theological matters and have no intention of pretending to appear as such. Hence I thought it best to let the cardinal's comments serve as a guide to the question of whether Liberation theology could be said to constitute good theology; and it is clear that, according to the official Catholic judgment, it does not. Moreover, and quite surprisingly, I find that his comments make points very similar in spirit, if not in detail, to those I tried to make in the last chapter while raising the six questions about the inappropriateness of treating social justice as a primary concern of religion. To repeat, for emphasis, what was said on page 58, the cardinal considers Liberation theology to be guilty of: reducing sin to social structures, of making the struggle for justice the whole essence of salvation, of reducing the gospel to a purely earthly gospel, of denying the transcendent character of the distinction between good and evil and (earlier on this page) of 'sacralizing' politics.

Despite the castigation by the Catholic church, however, I am prepared to concede that some elements of Liberation theology are rooted in the traditions of Christianity – not its mainstream perhaps, but a tradition, nonetheless. For example, it seems to be true that early Christians, that is, pre-Constantinian, first-century AD Christians, did share goods in common. Similarly, one may cite, say, the Methodist movement in eighteenth-century England, or the various sects in the English Civil War, as precursors to what one may regard as the tradition of non-violent Christian socialism, deeply embedded in English political life – which itself may, then, be perceived as a return to early Christianity. But to acknowledge this is not to admit that this strand ever became the mainstream of Christianity or that it amounted to the practically wholesale rejection or rewriting of the theological underpinnings of Christianity, especially its emphasis on the transcendent. Liberation theology seems to me to have gone well beyond what may be said to be justified in the name of this strand of tradition.

What I find particularly puzzling about Liberation theology is its claim that dualism of any sort was absent from early Christianity, until, that is, it came under European, specifically Greek, influence. Supposing, for the sake of the argument, that they are right, was what happened necessarily a bad thing? Isn't dualism – between the transcendental and the earthly, between the soul and the body, and so on – what gives religion its *raison d'être*, as a distinctive enterprise different from any other? Take away the transcendence of God and heaven, the immortality of the soul (as against the perishability of the body), the primacy of the felt need for salvation, of the kingdom to come (as against the one that is); and what would be left of religion that is not already contained in our other myriad mundane concerns? Even if one is made to concede that Judaism may not be dualistic on some of these counts, the conclusion one would be forced to come to is not, as Liberation theology claims, that dualism is an accretion to religion, but that Judaism may be an exception in this regard to the norm displayed by other religions. For Liberation theology to claim to be a *theology*, and yet to wish to reject dualism altogether, seems to betray a blind spot of significant proportions, even if – and I say 'if' – it shares that spot with Judaism. For it begins to hint at the distinct possibility that Liberation theologians perhaps do not understand religion in all its major manifestations, or else they disregard this understanding because they cannot, then, use it as an instrument of their political agenda. Nor do I quite understand their protest against the 'Europeanization' of early Christianity. Christianity, as we know it today, is very much a product of European culture; and has survived as an independent religion because of that factor, instead of being consigned to the status of a footnote in the history of the Hebrew tradition. The Liberation theologians' wish to revert to pre-European Christianity may be wholesome; but it would not alter the truth that 'European Christianity' may, in fact, be closer to the concept of religion, as exemplified in the world's great religions.

Finally, I am not sure that I particularly like the use of theology in the promotion of political ends, although the custom is time-honoured and widespread. Certainly, the masses may be persuaded more easily of the need for revolution, if the revolutionary ideology is administered with heavy doses of religion. But this precisely is treating religion as an 'opiate'.

Marx had noted how religion had functioned in this way in the past. But I wonder if he would have approved of Marxists exploiting the power of religion to advance the revolutionary cause. Liberation theologians, and those inspired by them, for example, Feminist theologians, Black theologians, Asian theologians and so on, claim – with some plausibility, in my opinion – that traditional theology, as often as not, provided the framework for the exploitation and the suppression of the rights of, say, the people of Latin America, of females, of blacks, of colonized Asians, as the case may be. If so, instead of rewriting theology to suit their own political purposes, would it not be more sensible for them to banish it from the political arena, letting it confine itself to properly religious issues, such as agape, devotion, salvation, the kingdom of God, *nirvāṇa*, and so on, instead of economic and political liberation? It has been said that only poison can be the antidote to poison. But is it really necessary to take that adage so seriously?

I hope that what I have said in this chapter, combined with the overall message of my questions in the preceding chapter, has succeeded in showing why it is wrong of Liberation theology to claim that social justice should be the entire, or even a main, concern of Christianity, or, for that matter, of religion in general. It seems to me that the dramatic changes in the political and economic conditions of the world that have occurred in the short time since Liberation theology came into prominence, themselves demonstrate why it is unwise to identify religion with political and economic goals, however urgent they may seem to be at a given time.

At the beginning of this chapter, I pointed out that there were, among others, three main factors that contributed to the emergence of Liberation theology: i) the influence of Marxist ideology, supposedly practised by the former Soviet block of socialist regimes; ii) the tyrannical military dictatorships in power in practically all of Latin America; and iii) the perception by Liberation theologians, and others, that Cuba, with its socialist set-up, had succeeded in improving the lot of its people – at least by contrast with the rest of Latin America. Now, with the collapse of the Soviet Union in 1991, all the former socialist countries are falling over backwards to embrace economic development and a market economy in an effort to enhance their economic and political well-being. Practically all the military regimes in Latin America have been replaced by democratic governments – not perfect democracies perhaps, but democracies, nonetheless. And Cuba, without the monetary and political support of the former Soviet Union, is in such economic and political disarray that the United States Coast Guard is barely able to contain the tide of refugees risking their lives to reach the shores of the United States. The former friends, foes, and fellow-travellers of Liberation theology are, thus, practically all gone. What has not gone away, however, is the poverty of the people and the economic disparities in Latin American society. What should Liberation theology do now? It cannot really be waging a revolutionary class struggle against popularly elected governments – or can it? At best, it seems to me, it can hope to constitute the voice of the political left. But that indirect role of religion has been around in Europe for a good two, or more, hundred years! Whatever its future, it seems that the short history of Liberation theology so far, already hints at the unwisdom of identifying religion with earthly and transient political and economic goals, rather than with other-worldly spiritual and moral missions.

6 Religion, Economic Development and Social Justice

So far in this book, I seem to have concentrated mainly on showing why it is a mistake to regard religion as a tool of social justice – at least in any direct way. In this chapter, I will, among other things, argue that religion, nonetheless, can play a very important, indirect, role in the attainment of social justice. Before I do that, however, I need to show what, if anything, economic development itself may have to do with social justice. What, I suppose, I do not have to do here is to make a case for the importance of economic development: that, it seems to me, has been done already by the large-scale conversion of world governments of all sorts to the capitalist model of free enterprise, economic development and a market economy. A very important indicator of this 'victory' may be the fact that, in June 1992, nearly 190 nations of the world gathered together for the Earth Summit in Rio de Janeiro. While adopting Agenda 21, a blueprint for arresting environmental degradation, they at the same time, adopted a comprehensive set of policies that would enable them to 'develop their economies'. The term used to describe this was 'sustainable development'.[1] Paradoxically, at the time, the-then President of the United States, George Bush, refused to sign the treatise, citing unacceptable costs to the United States as his reason for refusal. But the United States under the leadership of its new President, Bill Clinton, has, at last, endorsed the agreement. That meeting alone, not to mention the large-scale opening of doors to free enterprise and market economy across the world, makes economic development now the voluntarily adopted path of the world's governments towards the attainment of social justice, or, at least, of greater wealth.

What, then, is 'economic development'? The term usually signifies (a) economic growth, and (b) attendant 'modernization'. The former includes, 'rise in the total economic output of a society (or GNP)' *and* 'rise in per capita output'.[2] The latter refers to the 'institutional and cultural concomitants of economic growth under the conditions of sophisticated technology'.[3] It should be kept in mind that, although both 'growth' and 'modernization' are meant to be technical terms, supposedly value-neutral and descriptive, that's far from the case in most actual uses of the terms.

There is, for instance, a clear assumption that economic development, and therefore, growth and modernization, are desirable, because they constitute 'progress'. A society which is not developing economically is, therefore, deemed static; and, by the same token, a society's failure to modernize is indicative of its inefficiency, its lack of the requisite infrastructure and organization for progress – in short, of its 'primitive' or 'traditional', character. In what follows, I will, among other things, be examining some of the value-assumptions of these terms.

Let's start by asking, in the first place, why we ought to be talking at all of economic development in the context of social justice. The answer, presumably, is that the former is supposed to be a means to the latter: economic development is either a necessary and/or a sufficient condition of social justice. It is sometimes claimed that economic development not only solves the problem of production but also dissolves the problem of distribution. And perhaps this is so. But it is important, I think, to make some distinctions here, so that one can see somewhat more clearly the nature, and limits, of the alleged causal relationship. For it seems to me that economic growth need neither be a necessary nor a sufficient condition of certain aspects of social justice, notably the political ones. If a society, for example, is found wanting in relation to equal rights or basic liberties for its citizens, then the quest for justice in this society will be quite independent of its economic status or performance. One can imagine an economically well-developed nation denying human rights to its citizens. Conversely, one can point to a relatively poor society with a well-established egalitarian system of political and human rights. The latter example will have shown economic development not to be a necessary condition, and the former not a sufficient condition of the political aspects of social justice.

On the other hand, when it comes to economic necessities of the elementary kind, for example, the provision of ample food, nutrition, homes and jobs, and so on, it seems fairly obvious that economic growth, in the sense of increased production of the relevant goods and higher incomes for individuals, can have a directly instrumental role. The relationship between social justice and economic development, then, is not always the same, irrespective of context. It seems clear that in the context of what I called 'elementary' social justice, economic growth may be at least a necessary condition. It may, however, not be a sufficient condition. For if the political structure and/or the moral sensibilities of a society are not of the appropriate kind, then it may experience hunger and homelessness in spite of its affluence. Problems of production have to be separated from problems of distribution, and both from the lack of requisite moral sensibility and concern. When this is not done, economic development may be, simplistically, advocated as an end in itself. Such 'ideological' advocacy of economic development for its own sake, quite independently of the requirements of justice and good sense, has appropriately been called 'developmentalism'. And my point is that 'developmentalism' is quite distinct from economic development as a means to the attainment of social justice; and, therefore, one may with some reason, prescribe the latter without professing the former.

Since economic growth would seem to be more obviously instrumental in the amelioration of such conditions as hunger, malnutrition, homelessness and so on – phenomena *typically* associated with the poorer, 'developing' countries (euphemistically known as the Third World) – one might assume that the provision of social justice of this 'elementary' kind is a problem that, by and large, relates to the Third World. Although we will, for that reason, be speaking directly of the prospects, problems and pitfalls of development in the Third World, it should be pointed out that at least some of our observations may apply equally well to the 'first' and 'second' worlds. For poverty, unemployment, homelessness, or even hunger and malnutrition, have not altogether been eliminated from the richer Western societies. Practically every affluent society has managed to create 'sub-cultures' which have more in common with Third World societies than with the indigenous affluent majority. To that extent, the terms 'developed' and 'developing' may apply not so much to geographical regions (although by and large they certainly do so) as to levels of material affluence achieved by identifiable sectors of population within any society.

Some of my remarks in the second half of the last paragraph are partly intended to make the point that there is a clear sense in which the expression, the 'Third World' is an abstraction. It simply serves to pick out certain economic and political features common to a large number of countries in the world. Economically, it implies relative poverty; and, politically, it signifies that the country in question is not normally seen as belonging either to the capitalist or the formerly socialist group of Western nations. Another expression, 'North–South', is frequently used to make the same sort of distinction, especially the economic aspect of it. The 'South', then, signifies relative economic underdevelopment and poverty as contrasted with the relative affluence of the 'North'. It would be wrong to give the impression that the political basis of these contrasts is in any way unimportant. For our present purposes, however, the economic aspect requires special attention. And that, for the simple reason, that the terms 'Third World' and 'South', almost by definition, primarily signify poverty and underdevelopment.

As it turns out, the vast majority of countries in the world – certainly almost two-thirds of the world's present population – suffers from the deprivations of poverty (hence the occasional use of the term the 'two-thirds world'). From a political perspective, this fact that poverty is the lot of the bulk of humanity, acquires a special poignancy. But in the context of the consideration of social justice, that fact is not particularly relevant. The injustice of deprivation would be undesirable even if only a few people suffered it. The requirements of social justice will demand the elimination – or at least the amelioration – of the conditions associated with poverty, unless it happens to be everyone's lot. And if economic growth is the means to that end, then it goes without saying that at least the Third World needs to experience it. For, otherwise, we would be perpetuating the poverty and the attendant social injustice.

But since, here at least, economic development is recommended not as a goal in itself but as an instrument of social justice, care needs to be exercised to ensure that the means truly match the ends. Otherwise, unintended injustice may arise. It is not all that difficult to envisage situations where progress in achieving justice on some counts might itself create or give rise to deleterious side-effects, which may not be conducive to justice in society overall. A great deal of reflection and discrimination would seem to be called for. The following may be recommended as examples of factors requiring special consideration in the overall pursuit of economic growth:

1. Foremost among these, in my opinion, may be the need for flexibility in the choice of specific objectives and of the appropriate means. For, although it is in some ways convenient to speak of the Third World, or of developing countries, and so on, these expressions clearly do not refer to a culturally, politically, or even economically, homogeneous population. What may be suitable for one identifiable population group or country may be utterly unsuitable for another, either for economic or political reasons or for larger reasons of justice. Care, therefore, would need to be exercised in identifying the needs and characteristics of each distinctive population group, rather than lumping all of them together under one theoretical or ideological label – whatever the ancestry of the latter. For example, it will have to be judged whether a specific country or region primarily needed increased agricultural production, reduction in the size, or direction of movement of the population, or the redistribution of land or of food, possibly already produced in abundance. It might well be found in a given case that a bit of each of the above was required or appropriate – in which case, their relative priority would have to be determined, which in its turn would establish the criteria for the choice of appropriate means.

This sensitivity to the needs and characteristics of identifiable population groups and a strong commitment to make these the primary determinants of choice, is, I think, very important. For any failure in this respect might prove ultimately counter-productive to the goals of social justice.

2. A special case of this general requirement of sensitivity entails the choice of what I have elsewhere called 'sensitive technology'.[4] For most parts of the developing world, for example, labour-intensive rather than capital-intensive technology would seem to be more appropriate, simply because they may have an abundance of labour and an acute shortage of capital. Heavy industry, with a disproportionately high use of automated technology, would be likely to cause unemployment or underemployment and a possible drift of population in unwanted directions. The technology chosen should, as far as possible, be capable of preserving the ecological balance of the region concerned, such balance to include avoidance of unnecessary urbanization and its after-effects, not to mention pollution of the environment. Also, the scale of industry and the technology chosen should show a clear awareness of the natural resources of the region concerned. There should be an attempt to eschew large-scale industry, with its attendant centralization and bureaucratization. A sensitive diffusion of the productive capacity and distributive machinery should be aimed at. The need for the adoption of 'sensitive technology', as just outlined, may be important in its own right; but, especially in the context of social justice, it seems to me to be imperative. For, otherwise, unintended injustices may arise.

3. As we have seen, economic development, almost by definition, seems to include attendant 'modernization'. Now, to some extent, the very possibility of growth may require a certain degree of 'rationalization' of supporting social structures and mores. Efficient production of goods and services may be said to need efficiency-oriented cultural and institutional infrastructures. And if development alone, irrespective of anything else, were the objective, one might quite rightly insist on imposing the appropriate orientation on the society in question. But if the objective is social justice, it would be quite legitimate to ask whether the insistence on modernization might itself constitute injustice of a subtler kind. For modernization, strictly speaking, entails 'Westernization'. And if the intended recipient of social justice is a non-Western society, with its own distinctive culture, tradition and religious outlook, then the very attempt at modernization might involve inflicting injustice. Since justice includes in its scope 'the bases of self-respect', as we saw when talking about Rawls in Chapter 2, preservation of a society's sense of its distinctive identity is very much part of justice; and anything that erodes or undermines its cultural or national identity is

likely to be perceived as threats to its sovereignty. It is of the very essence
of justice that an individual or society freely chooses its own happiness.
Imposing Westernization, or anything else, is paternalistic and thus contrary to the spirit of justice. More pertinently, when the concomitants of
economic development are seen to threaten the religious and cultural identity
of a society or nation, resistance in the form of religious fundamentalism
or national chauvinism is created, which generate intolerance, hostility,
and even war. The result, then, is not justice, but its opposite. An indiscriminate pursuit of modernity can thus be counter-productive to the aim
of social justice. There is, however, more to the respect for cultural and
national identity of people. There is a strong case, I think, for the view that
the retention of cultural and national diversity is demanded by considerations
of dignity and respect for other cultures. Additionally, it is probable that
the continued survival of the human race may be rendered more likely by
the retention of competing lifestyles than by encouraging the growth of
a 'monoculture'. If there is a variety of lifestyles, then in the event of a
catastrophe, natural or man-made, it is more likely that at least one of
them will survive. When the whole human population becomes culturally
homogeneous, we may, in survival terms, be getting into an all-or-none
game. Cultural diversity in the human population has the same logic as
that of biodiversity in nature.

We have so far looked at the role of economic development in securing
what we earlier called 'elementary' social justice, primarily in the Third
World. As we move from 'elementary' to 'full-blown' social justice, and,
therefore, from the third to the 'first' world, or the affluent societies, it
would seem that economic growth need no longer be regarded as a primary instrument in the pursuit of justice. For these societies are rich already. If hunger, malnutrition or homelessness still persist in sections of
these societies, then it should be clear that what is required is the political
will to distribute the goods more equitably. And yet in these countries in
the West there seems to be a tacit assumption that economic growth ought
to be pursued for its own sake, and forever. None of them seems to
question the need for economic growth. And yet such questioning is ab-
solutely essential. Why should it be assumed that getting richer – which
is what continued economic growth amounts to – is, in any sense, automatically a means to greater social justice? The socialist assumption was
that the increased wealth produced through economic development would
be evenly distributed among the masses by the state. Likewise, liberalism
– both its contractarian and utilitarian varieties – assumes that the liberal
state would promulgate legislation that would ensure that the country's
wealth would be distributed according to just principles, enunciated as

parts of their overall theories of justice. The connection between economic development and social justice, then, is not necessary, but contingent on intervention by the state, in order to bring about a just state of affairs. Capitalism, and libertarianism, on the other hand, are guided by the belief – explicitly or implicitly held – in what has come to be known as the 'spread-effect' or the 'trickle-down effect' of economic growth.

It is important to examine not only the empirical validity of this notion of the 'spread-effect' as a means to social justice, but also of the very idea of economic growth as progress, especially in the context of social justice. Here are some observations that I believe need to be made.

1. The 'spread-effect' or the 'trickle-down effect' is, in my opinion, at best, unobtainable beyond a certain limit and, at worst, completely spurious as an instrument of social justice. It can be argued that in the more affluent societies of the West, although wealth is concentrated in the hands of a few individuals or families, everyone in these societies is relatively better off compared to individuals in the poorer countries. And this would be hard to deny. But whether this phenomenon is the result of the so-called spread-effect or of two centuries of liberal thinking and social legislation is altogether a different matter. More importantly, despite such legislation and the practice of 'welfare economics', pockets of poverty – including even hunger and malnutrition, not to mention homelessness, significant degrees of unemployment and lack of adequate housing – still exist in the West. The coexistence side by side of immense material wealth, on the one hand, and hunger, homelessness and lack of adequate health-care, on the other, makes the injustice of the latter more, rather than less, stark and shocking.

Proponents of economic growth as the eventual benefactor of all sometimes use the analogy of a marching column to explain how everyone is ultimately better off as a result of continuing growth. 'The ranking of the column reflects the income distribution, which stays more or less unchanged over time, as the column as a whole advances. The people at the head are usually "the first to wheel in a new direction. The last rank keeps its distance from the first, and the distance between them does not lessen. But as the column advances, the last rank does eventually reach and pass the point which the first rank had passed some time before. . . . The people in the rear cannot, without breaking rank and rushing ahead, reach where the van *is*, but, since the whole column is moving forward, they can hope in due course to reach where the van *was*." '[5] But, this analogy fails to take account of the social costs of growth and its built-in frustrations for 'the last rank'. The social effects of 'crowding', 'screening' and 'auction' ensure that by the time the majority reaches the income levels enjoyed by the 'elite' some time ago, suburbia has been spoilt, the beaches polluted and the roadways jammed.[6] If there is still a place left without these problems, then the 'proletariat' is sure to have been priced out of the race for possession. 'Positional goods' do not follow the logic of 'private goods' in terms of satisfaction; and so by the time 'all' (or almost all) are enabled by the growing material economy to compete for the former, they are usually either not worth pursuing or else impossible to get. What may be attainable by each of us, individually, is not attainable by all, collectively: this seems to be the 'logic' of positional goods.[7]

2. Quite apart from the chimeral nature of the supposed benefits, for all, of economic growth, it is possible to argue that it is morally offensive – certainly contrary to the spirit of justice – to consign a certain percentage of a human population to a situation where they are forever trying to catch up with the 'elite'. Justice, in order to be made available universally, may have to be politically 'engineered', rather than left to the caprice of individual free enterprise.

3. The last remark may seem to suggest that perhaps the socialist alternative of revolutionary redistribution of resources would be more likely to bring about a fairer apportioning of goods – 'at one stroke', as it were. But it would be naive to be unmindful of the inherent costs of a revolution. The violence – physical and psychological – that a revolution inevitably involves, may itself be too heavy a price to pay. Besides, the loss of incentive, and the emergence of state control in place of individual liberties have to be taken into account. It may also be argued that the orthodox socialist alternative merely replaces 'economic elitism' – where the vanguard consists of the profit-seeking entrepreneur – by 'political elitism' – where the vanguard is constituted by the power-seeking party intellectual and manager. If the former is characterized by indifference to social welfare, the latter besports a degree of paternalism and the loss of individual liberties that do not exactly go hand in hand with the idea of justice. The rejection of this alternative by the formerly socialist states in the former Soviet Union and Eastern Europe may well be a vindication of the point just made. This would seem to leave liberalism as the ideology best equipped to distribute the increased wealth resulting from economic development according to its own principles of justice. We will take up this point, again, later in this chapter and in the rest of the book. For the moment, we continue with our critical observations.

4. As is well known, a strong case has been made against the philosophy of continued economic growth by the Club of Rome, primarily on empirical and environmental grounds. And ecologists across the world continue to draw attention to the environmental pollution and depletion of resources endemic to economic growth and industrialization. Additionally,

Hirsch has produced what seems to me to be a convincing account of the 'social limits to growth',[8] briefly referred to earlier. But although all these indictments of growth have received widespread attention, the political and economic 'establishments' throughout the world still pursue growth, as if they had heard nothing. Or, have they?

Perhaps this is the appropriate place to return to the question of how religion can, after all, play an indirect, but nonetheless important, role in the context of economic development and its potential for social justice.

For a start, it can do so by challenging the view, implicit, at least in what I called 'developmentalism', namely, that getting rich or richer is in itself a virtue. No religion seems to have taken that position: indeed, it is poverty that has been hailed by practically every religion as a virtue. Continued economic growth and the needless exploitation of natural resources may be an understandable position for capitalism to take, in that there is nothing higher for it to appeal to: the individual pursuit of happiness and the corporate pursuit of profit must be continued, wherever it may lead to. But religion is not prevented from taking a 'paternalistic' view and saying, 'This must stop!'. I ought to add, as a reminder in case one was needed, that quite apart from the value placed on poverty by all religions, the growth of capitalism itself may have been made possible by the 'rational asceticism' inherent in the Protestant ethic. More will be written about this in Chapters 9 and 10. For the moment I simply wish to emphasize the need for religion to counteract developmentalism and all that goes with it.

At this point, I might be asked: But what does this have to do with justice? It might be conceded – if it is – that if religion succeeds in counteracting capitalism, and thus the ever-continuing growth, with its deleterious social and environmental ill effects, that might indeed be a good thing for the planet and its population. But how does this serve the cause of justice? I think it would do so by stopping or minimizing the 'usurpation' of the scant resources of the poor and the politically weak across the world who cannot stop the juggernaut of developmentalism in its incessant march. And that applies also to the cause of defenceless species and their habitats. (I have said before, in Chapter 1, that I do not find the idea of animal rights incoherent, although I am aware of the thinking of those who do.) Economic development does not present a level playing field: those who own the capital and wield political power are the greater beneficiaries of the fruits of development; and they benefit at the expense of the poor and powerless. This is just as true within a nation as across nations. The non-renewable natural resources of the poor, such as minerals, forests, and the like, are bought cheaply to make goods for the rich. If religion were to succeed in stopping, or even significantly curbing, unnecessary economic growth, it would help curb the phenomenon of the rich getting richer at the expense of the poor. Additionally, it would also secure greater justice across generations, by conserving these scarce resources for use by future generations.

The other important way in which religion can advance the cause of social justice is by promoting moral and spiritual values that neither capitalism nor its philosophical allies – libertarianism and liberalism – bring with them. The virtues of love, compassion, altruism and self-sacrifice, traditionally promoted by religion, help, at the very least, to soften the harshness of capitalist competition and to build humane communities out of selfish individuals ceaselessly pursuing their own ends. There is little doubt that classical capitalism itself saw religion as providing a much needed counterweight to its own doctrine of individual free enterprise. According to no less a figure than Adam Smith,

> (Men) could safely be trusted to pursue their own self-interest without undue harm to the community not only because of the restrictions imposed by the law, but also because they were subject to built-in restraint derived from morals, religion, custom and education.[9]

And while J. S. Mill found the idea of a society held together merely by mutual pecuniary interests, essentially repulsive,[10] he did not fail to notice that religion served as 'a supplement to human laws, a more cunning sort of police'.[11]

The successors of Adam Smith among economists may seem to have become oblivious of the role of religion and morality in the establishment of a just social order. According to Irving Kristol, for instance, 'The idea of bourgeois virtue has been eliminated from (Milton) Friedman's conception of bourgeois society.'[12] Amartya Sen is of the opinion that 'as-if-altruistic',[13] as against really altruistic, behaviour is all that is needed. But, whatever the failure of modern economists in this respect, this accusation will be hard to sustain against sociologists: they have been very cognizant of the importance of religion and the attendant morality in holding society together and keeping it caring. As Hirsch says, 'The functional aspect of religion has always been prominent in the sociological approach: Comte stressing the contribution of belief and ritual to social solidarity and Durkheim the role of religion in inducing participation in social life.'[14] Quite independently of the positions of economists and sociologists, however, it seems to be the case that the individualistic, rationalistic base of the market might have, over the years, undermined the religious basis of social organization. Social obligation no longer seems to have the power that it might have had in the past. For capitalism to be conducive to, or even compatible with, social justice, however, morality in the form of a social and political conscience may be necessary. And that being so, religion, once again, needs to reclaim its traditional role in society as the basis of community and the source of moral and spiritual values.

But it is not just because of the intimate connection between morality and religion that the latter becomes important. There may be an additional, and perhaps even more, important reason. As Peter Berger says, '. . . Man does *not* live by bread alone. He also needs the life-giving and meaning-giving sustenance that no "naturalist" view of the world can provide. If you will, man needs religion, and if that is so, no technocratic design for human life can be finally satisfactory.'[15] In other words, human beings need myths, a 'myth' being 'any set of ideas that infuses transcendent meaning into the lives of men – transcendent with regard to the routine and selfish concerns of ordinary life'.[16] It can be argued, convincingly, I think, that individuals with this sense of transcendence may, on the whole, be much better equipped to create a just society than a bunch of them unable to see beyond their immediate economic goals.

Apart from serving as a source of morality in general, religion may have a special role – an indirect, but perhaps indispensable one, again – if economic development is to lead to social justice. For, as Hirsch points out, the pursuit of individual self-interest, the basis of capitalist enterprise, does not by itself lead to the social good: 'Rather than pursuit of self-interest contributing to the social good, pursuit of the social good contributes to the satisfaction of self-interest. The difficulty is that the latter pursuit needs to be deliberately organized under existing standards and instincts of personal behavior,'[17] a task not easily accomplished without restoring religion to its traditional, pivotal, place in society. It is religion, then, that must help re-establish the primacy of altruistic behaviour and the spirit of community, as also of goals higher than material wealth and physical well-being.

There is, finally, one other way in which religion helps the cause of social justice. Every religious tradition has encouraged the doing of 'good works', such as building hospitals, orphanages, drug rehabilitation centres, and homes for the homeless and refugees, etc. Traditionally, these works have been inspired by a sense of fellow feeling, compassion, charity, and so on, and not by the need to build just economic and political institutions. But whatever the source of inspiration, these works have always played an immensely important role in mitigating the pain and suffering of those who have been dealt with harshly by an uncaring nature or by unjust social and political regimes. These good works, then, – 'the fruits of the spirit', one might call them – are not, by any means, the least important contributions of religion towards the creation of a just and humane social order.

7 Modernity, Nationalism and Religious Fundamentalism

The two terms most commonly used to describe the various forms of religious activism evident around the world today are 'religious fundamentalism' and 'religious nationalism'. Some might prefer to use just one of these as an all-inclusive 'umbrella-word'.[1] I am of the opinion that both are needed, each in its appropriate context; for each of these has connotations which the other does not; and, if the resurgence of religion, globally, is to be captured in its entirety, as far as possible, then both sets of the connotations need to be retained. I wish to start by talking about 'fundamentalism' first, postponing the consideration of 'nationalism' and 'modernity' for a little while.

'Fundamentalism' and 'fundamentalist' are terms used so frequently these days that it can be fairly safely concluded that some of these uses must, in fact, be abuses. But, beyond that, there may be other good reasons for suggesting that this term, 'fundamentalism', ought to be avoided altogether as a characterization of the many forms of the resurgence of religion outside the West, perhaps even outside America. In its primary sense, 'fundamentalism' meant 'a recent movement in American Protestantism in opposition to modernistic tendencies, re-emphasizing as fundamental to Christianity the inerrancy of the Scriptures, Biblical miracles, especially the virgin birth and physical resurrection of Christ and substitutional atonement'.[2] Fundamentalism in this sense is certainly alive in America today, perhaps even thriving. But it should be clear that no Muslim, Jew, Hindu or Buddhist can be a fundamentalist in the primary sense just spoken of, for they are not even Christians, far less American Protestants. By extension, however, the term can be used to refer to a similar phenomenon in these other religions, if they contain individuals or groups of people who proclaim the inerrancy of their own scriptures, doctrines, traditions or myths. And there certainly are such instances to be found in them. What needs to be pointed out, however, is that, especially when it comes to countries outside the West – whether Islamic, Hindu, Buddhist or Jewish – it is the pejorative sense of the term that is most commonly used, sometimes explicitly, but often only in an insinuating way. One Muslim scholar, not wishing to have himself or other Islamic religious activists described as fundamentalist, pointed out that the reason he objected to that description was that the term referred to those who hold 'an intolerant, self-righteous, and narrowly dogmatic religious literalism'.[3] But that is not at all how he viewed himself or some of the other Muslims described as fundamentalist. A pejorative word does not help the task either of describing or explaining.

There are good reasons for thinking, too, that the many different kinds of religious-political activism across the world may not all be fundamentalist: some of them are much more accurately described as instances of what Juergensmeyer calls 'religious nationalism'. Certainly, looking across the world, it seems that what is happening in India, Sri Lanka, Iran, Tajikistan, Nagorno-Karabakh or Bosnia-Herzegovina is more the upsurge of religious nationalism than the emergence of fundamentalism: at best, the 'fundamentalists' in these countries, where there are any, may simply be a sub-group of the more numerous religious nationalists.

Thus while I appreciate the reasons why 'fundamentalism', and its cognates, have to be used with a great deal of caution and foreboding, I still think, on the whole, that such use may be unavoidable. In *Fundamentalisms Observed*, editors Martin E. Marty and R. Scott Appleby advance several plausible reasons for settling on this controversial term to describe the 14 very different examples of religious activism occurring in very different parts of the world. I do not wish to reiterate all those arguments here; but the one I found most persuasive is the very first one given by them: namely, that '"fundamentalism" is here to stay'.[4] Almost all the indications seem to be in favour of that presumption – at least at this point in time.

Mindful of the differences among these 14 examples of activism, and of the consequent difficulties in precisely defining, 'fundamentalism', Marty and Appleby acknowledge, without explaining, that the similarities among the 14 may well be appropriately described in terms of the Wittgensteinian notion of 'family resemblances', that is, a network of similarities, criss-crossing and sometimes overlapping, among them, rather than a set of common features characterizing them all. The best way to view this 'network' may be provided by using the verb 'fight' and some of its customary prepositional suffixes. These family resemblances that justify the use of a single term, 'fundamentalism', then, to describe all of them are the following:[5]

1. *Fighting back*: All of these movements are 'militant', and are setting themselves up against forces which might have so far considered themselves victors already.
2. *Fighting for*: They may be fighting for 'a worldview' central to which are views about intimate aspects of life, such as family, gender, sex roles, the nurturing and education of children, and so on.

3. *Fight with*: The instrument or weapon they choose to fight with, typically, is the evocation of a kind of nostalgia for an actual or presumed past, 'actual or imagined ideal original conditions and concepts'.
4. *Fight against*: They are fighting against enemies whom they regard as 'the agents of assault on all that is held dear': the enemies, then, may be the 'infidel', 'the modernizer' or even 'the compromiser', who wishes to take the middle ground.
5. *Fight under*: Typically, they fight 'under God', as in the case of the theistic religions, or else, 'under the signs of some transcendent reference', as in the case of non-theistic religions or sects.

'Fundamentalism', as elaborated above, seems to be a comprehensive enough term and ought, therefore, to be able to designate all forms of religious activism encountered round the world. Why, then, do I wish to retain the use of the other term, that is, 'religious nationalism' as well? Before attempting an answer to that question, let me, first, indicate how this term, and certain others integral to its meaning, ought to be understood. Since I borrow this term from Juergensmeyer, it is best, I think, to use his definitions for this term as well as the ones it presupposes. Here they are in his own words:

> By the *state*, I mean the locus of authority and decision-making within a geographical region. By the *nation*, I mean a community of people associated with a particular political culture and territory that possesses autonomous political authority. A *nation-state* is a modern form of nationhood in which a state's authority systematically pervades and regulates an entire nation, whether through democratic or totalitarian means. The modern nation-state is morally and politically justified by a concept of *nationalism*, by which I mean not only the xenophobic extremes of patriotism but also the more subdued expressions of identity based on shared assumptions regarding why a community constitutes a nation and why the state that rules it is legitimate.[6] [He adds, later:] . . . The term *religious nationalism* in today's parlance, therefore, means the attempt to link religion and the nation-state. This is a new development in the history of nationalism, and it immediately raises the question of whether it is possible: whether what we in the West think of as a modern nation – a unified, democratically controlled system of economic and political administration – can in fact be accommodated within religion.[7]

The answer given by the religious nationalists is an emphatic 'yes': not only can the nation be accommodated within religion; it must be. It is wrong to keep them apart. Religious nationalists, then, may be – are – all sorts of other things as well; but, first and foremost, they are the enemies of secular nationalism and of the separation of religion and state. It should now be seen that fundamentalism and religious nationalism, although they may often be allies, have quite different missions. Fundamentalism is primarily a movement to correct what is perceived as the distorted nature of religiosity and of 'family values' prevalent today; religious nationalism is a movement to correct the nature of the state or of politics. The former is a religious movement, but the latter is a political movement, with religion at its centre. Wherever both are in evidence, they are natural allies: the gains of one are perceived to be the gains of the other, too. This may change over time, especially if the nationalists succeed in achieving their objectives, and, then, for pragmatic reasons, no longer want to go the way of the fundamentalists. This may, to some extent, be in evidence in contemporary Iran where President Rafsanjani is no longer the favourite of the fundamentalists among the Islamic clergy in Iran. But, initially, the alliance is very logical.

But alliance is not identity; and, therefore, if one is to understand the recent resurgence of religious activism round the world in its entirety, I think we need both terms. This should be evident if we consider, for example, that in America today there is no overt movement of religious nationalism, perhaps only because the constitutional separation of religion and state here discourages talking in those terms; yet no one who is knowledgeable will wish to deny that fundamentalism here is quite strong. By contrast, in India and in Sri Lanka we encounter powerful religious nationalisms – of Hindu nationalism in the former and of Singhalese Buddhist nationalism in the latter. And it is for that reason that traditional animosities between Hindus and Muslims in India, and Buddhist Singhalese and Hindu Tamils in Sri Lanka, have been heightened so as to become explosive forces of conflict. When it comes to fundamentalism, however, I am not sure that either of these countries provides clear examples of that. For neither Hinduism nor Buddhism, being non-doctrinaire, non-credal religions, lend themselves easily to a fundamentalist reassertion of dogma directed against 'modernizers'. What is causing, or intensifying, inter-religious conflict in these countries is the demand by the majority religious communities to abandon secular nationalism and make India a Hindu state and Sri Lanka a Buddhist one, thus causing a backlash of violent protest from the sizeable minority religious communities – Muslims, Sikhs and (in places) Christians in India; and Tamil Hindus and (to a lesser extent) Muslims and Christians in Sri Lanka. In Islamic countries, however, both fundamentalism and religious nationalism are in evidence – the former challenging modernist interpretations of Islamic doctrines and practices, the latter fighting the secular nationalism of these countries, particularly noticeable in Egypt, Algeria, Tunisia and Sudan.

But, as I said earlier, these two movements – fundamentalism and religious nationalism – wherever they both exist, are generally allies. And they are allies, because many of the contemporary phenomena and trends that each is fighting against overlap with those of the other: they, therefore, have, or feel they have, common enemies. Some of these relate to instances of perceived injustice in the past, others to real or perceived political and economic injustices and inequalities being suffered now and yet others to real or imagined threats to their religion, culture or 'nation' that they see as possibilities for the future. But, in a sense, this way of speaking of injustices of the past and present and of fears for the future is misleading; for they are not separated from each other. On the contrary, the actual or perceived injustices of the past and the present may not only exacerbate, but even cause the fears about the future. Thus, it is more accurate to say that all of them together may constitute a hazy but powerful notion of 'the enemy', which needs to be resisted and fought. This 'jumble of resentments', however, can be seen to have some distinct aspects which I will now try to outline.

The first of these could be called 'the fear of anomie'. As civilization becomes more and more global, it threatens the loss of identity for more or less distinct communities. Religious nationalism is, among other things, a reassertion of the recognizable identities of peoples – as often religious as ethnic or tribal. As globalization gathers momentum, it inevitably triggers a reaction in the opposite direction. Both trends seem to be identifiable round the world. On the one hand, we see a deliberate seeking out of economic and political structures which can best be described as enlarged 'federal' institutions, for example, the European Community, the North American Free Trade Agreement, the Association of South East Asian Nations and the ever tantalizing idea of a pan-Arab Islamic federal entity, and so on. On the other hand, we have witnessed the breaking up of the former Soviet Union and the former Yugoslavia, and are aware of stresses and strains within the unity of the EEC, and the recurring possibility, for instance, of India's disintegration as a federal republic. Certainly outside the West, and often inside it, as in Bosnia-Herzegovina and Ireland, for example, the reassertion of identity is anchored to a religion, and finds expression as religious nationalism.

The second of these aspects, in evidence practically everywhere outside the West, is a rebellion against post-colonial Western dominance exercised by capitalism and its tools: big money, big corporations and the power they enjoy over less well-off developing countries. Western governments in this context are seen as promoters of capitalism, which they certainly are. Even international institutions such as the World Bank and the International Monetary Fund are seen as being, in practice, merely the tools of capitalism and as neo-colonial forms of Western dominance, simply because decision-making in them is effectively controlled by the rich Western governments. Fundamentalists may or may not be concerned, or even seriously cognizant, of this factor. But to the religious nationalist, this clearly comes across as an affront that is barely distinguishable from the colonial domination of the not-so-distant past. Especially in the case of Islamic religious nationalism, an extra dimension of bitterness is added by memories of the long-standing rivalry and conflict between Islam and Christianity: the Crusades, the *Jihads*, the conquest of large parts of the West during the Ottoman empire and its eventual defeat by the Christian imperialist powers of the West. Although this element is of special significance in the context of religious nationalism within Islam, it is not entirely absent in the non-Islamic countries. For there is hardly a country in the world which did not suffer the injustices and humiliation inflicted by colonialism. But not just that: there is no religion in the world that did not lose adherents to Christianity, protected as it was by colonial, imperial power and able to use the wealth of its churches. Because colonialism and the missionary churches of Christianity were partners in the Western domination of the rest of the world, it is sometimes difficult to tell when anti-Western resentments are directed against Christianity, the religion of the West, and when they have a political or economic focus. And it is this history of partnership, too, that aids the alliance between non-Western fundamentalism and religious nationalism, despite the fact that the two sets of movements have distinct purposes.

The third aspect, although somewhat overlapping with the first, is the fear of the growth of a 'monoculture' generated by modernity and its technological tools. This threatens national, regional and tribal cultures based on traditional ways of life. The phenomenon of teenagers across the world preferring to wear blue jeans, listening to pop-music and dancing in dazzling discos may thrill teenagers themselves as heralding their entry into the modern world, the fast emerging global culture of the young among the middle classes. But it does not go down well with the older generations of people in non-Western cultures, because they see it as threatening the continued health, not to mention the continuing enrichment, of their own music, dance, art, ritual and religion. Modernity in this form, however, is more likely to be anathema to fundamentalists than to religious nationalists. For the younger among the nationalists may well have imbibed this youth culture themselves. Equally, the nationalists, especially the younger ones among them, may not be averse to modernity in its political or economic forms – democracy, bureaucratic forms of organization, market economics and the technological tools that go with them. Indeed, the nationalists are frequently skilful in the use of technology in shaping public opinion, in the acquisition of wealth and of political power, so much so that they may seem to be not unlike their 'Yuppie' counterparts in the West. Some of the younger activists among the supporters of the Bharatiya Janata Party, the Hindu nationalist party in India, for example, have indeed been called 'Scuppies', or 'Saffron-Clad Yuppies'.[8] What distinguishes them from Yuppies in the West may be nothing more than the saffron robes they wear as marks of their Hindu nationalism.

These three 'aspects', as I called them, are clusters of phenomena, which either fundamentalists or religious nationalists, or both, oppose and fight against. As I tried to indicate above, one or more of these aspects, or parts of them, may be the focus of opposition more by fundamentalists than religious nationalists, or the other way round. But, by and large, they overlap, thus providing the common 'enemy' for both groups. I do not, however, mean to suggest that the targets of opposition outlined above, by any means, constitute an exhaustive list. And even in relation to any specific phenomenon referred to above, the opposition from either kind of religious activism admits of many nuances and degrees of intensity. For example, fundamentalists are less likely to be tolerant of religious pluralism than nationalists. And this is perfectly understandable. If one is inhospitable to 'modernizing' influences and interpretations within one's own religion – as fundamentalists invariably are – then it is unlikely that he or she will be willing to embrace an altogether different religion. But nationalists, being primarily political creatures, are likely to be more pragmatic and, thus, at least in their rhetoric, likely to come across as being tolerant of pluralism, especially if they are citizens of a religiously pluralistic nation, such as India, for example. The typical supporter of the Bharatiya Janata Party, for example, is likely to pay at least lip-service to the desirability of the existence of religious minorities, such as the Muslims, Sikhs or Christians in India, while maintaining at the same time that, as a nation-state, India ought to be Hindu rather than secular in character. It may, indeed, be claimed, as it is in India by the leaders of the BJP, that the Muslims, Sikhs and Christians, while forming different communities religiously, are all products of 'Hindu culture', and, therefore, culturally, Hindus after all. This spirit of inclusiveness, I think, will be unacceptable to Hindu fundamentalists, if such creatures do indeed exist. Fundamentalism and religious pluralism do not go together: religious nationalism and pluralism just might, howsoever uncomfortable this coexistence may be, in practice. It ought to be noted here that only American fundamentalists and some evangelical groups abstained from the recent meeting in Chicago of the Parliament of the World's Religions.

Can fundamentalists and religious nationalists be said to be anti-Western? Evidently, Western activists cannot be said to be anti-Western: that just would not make sense. Non-Western activism, however, can frequently be anti-Western. If the details of our discussion of the three aspects above is recalled, then it should not be difficult to see that the features of the second and third aspects – namely, neo-colonial dominance and the 'monoculture' generated by modern technology and its tools – clearly have their origins and controlling power located in the West. And, for that reason, anyone resentful of those features would tend to be anti-Western. But even the first aspect – namely, the globalization of human civilization and the fear of 'anomie' that it generates may also be seen to be a consequence of Westernization; and can, for the same reason, be the target of opposition. Thus it is fairly safe to say, I think, that, by and large, non-Western religious activism – whether of the fundamentalist or nationalist variety – may, sometimes, be anti-Western as well. Care, however, needs to be taken to remember, again, that the focus of religious fundamentalism is different from that of nationalism; and, hence, no sweeping generalizations about either group regarding their possible anti-Western orientation is likely to be entirely correct. Nationalists, as I mentioned above, may frequently be quite comfortable with modern Western institutions, such as democracy, centralized bureaucracy and market-oriented economic organization. In their anti-Westernism, then, wherever it is a factor, that is, they are likely to be 'picky', accepting some features of Westernization but rejecting others.

In the discussion above I have had to refer to the term 'modern' or 'modernity' a few times, but only in passing. I now proceed to a somewhat more sustained and detailed treatment of the term. No one would be surprised if I were to say that 'modern' (and its cognates) is one of the most frequently used terms, especially in the social sciences. And yet, while we can all roughly delineate what it means in a particular context, its precise sense tends to be elusive, for the simple reason that even the descriptive sense of this term, not to mention its many pejorative nuances, is hard to determine.

The fact is that the word 'modern' (including its cognates: 'modernity', 'modernization', 'modernizer' and 'modernism' etc.) carries a multiplicity of meanings. Even in its basic sense, it is not only contrasted with 'ancient' but also with 'archaic' – two rather different things altogether. When contrasted with 'traditional', it can have, at least, three very distinct senses, depending on the particular academic discipline chosen as the home of its primary use. In economics, for example, a form of production is not modern if it happens to be pre-industrial and the technology used is outdated, and, therefore, almost by definition, 'inefficient'. In this context, then, no form of production, or technology, can be modern unless it is conducive to 'economic growth'. We have already seen that, in the political context 'modern' may, among other things, signify a pro-attitude towards democratic institutions, bureaucratic forms of organization, freedom of the press and other media, and so on. In social anthropology, however, a society is traditional, and not modern, if it displays certain attitudes: for example, if its thinking is 'unreflective' and 'unsystematic'; when it is governed by motives other than explanation and control; when it does not have the counterparts of specialists in theory-making; and, finally, when its thinking displays an uncritical attitude to established beliefs and concepts.[9] It should be noted that the word 'traditional' in this context is itself a somewhat recently introduced substitute for 'primitive', which was found to have disparaging, pejorative connotations. For that reason, the term 'traditional' typically refers to African tribal societies and their equivalents in America, Australia and elsewhere.

In spite of the diversity, almost confusion, of meanings attached to the word, 'modern', however, there is no doubt that, for all practical purposes, it has come to mean 'Western'. It may simply be owing to the fact that the distinction between modern and traditional – in whichever specific sense – was drawn by Western intellectuals and theorists; or because, as a matter of fact, practically all the concrete examples of modern institutions, theories and technologies happen to have originated in, and are to be found primarily in, the West. But whatever the explanation, the truth is that it is no longer possible to separate 'modernization' from 'Westernization'.

In our earlier discussion in this chapter, I have already indicated – albeit briefly – in which of these many senses of 'modern' either fundamentalism or nationalism could be said to be anti-modern. But the derivative of 'modern' that seems to me to be of the greatest interest in the present context – and which I have not dealt with at any length so far – is 'modernism'. This term has been used by recent writers[10] on religion and politics to refer to 'secular ideologies that dominate modern cultures',[11] or 'the ideology of individualism and a relativist view of moral values'.[12] This distinction between 'modernity' (and its other derivatives mentioned earlier) and 'modernism' enables one to make a very important point. And that is this. Religious nationalists, it may now be said are 'anti-modernists', without being 'anti-modern'. This is very crucial. As Juergensmeyer, using 'Anthony Gidden's frame of reference', says:

Nationalism, from his point of view, is a condition for entry into a modern world political and economic system based on the building blocks of nation-states. It is unthinkable that a political or economic entity can function without some relationship to large patterns of international commerce and political alignment, and this relationship requires strong centralized control on a national level. Because movements for religious nationalism aim at strengthening national identities, they can be seen as highly compatible with the modern system.[13]

So religious nationalism is not anti-modern, but antimodernist: it rejects only what it regards as the 'perverse and alienating features of modernism',[14] some of which we discussed while talking about the three aspects of the 'jumble of resentments' earlier. It should be easily seen that religious fundamentalists, too, are anti-modernists, and emphatically so, whether or not they are anti-modern.

It will be recalled that I have described fundamentalism and religious nationalism as allies, although their primary missions are different. I also said earlier that their alliance is made possible by the fact that some of their objectives overlap. It should now be clear where this overlap is most obvious and significant: it lies in the fact that both forms of activism are against the ideology of modernism, comprising secularism, individualism, amoralism, the attendant hedonism, the emphasis on rights and the disavowal of righteousness and of transcendent purposes and goals. Both groups are convinced that secularism is wrong: states, according to them, must be based on religious laws and values. Individuals, according to them, cannot have any identity outside and independent of the community, church, *sangha* or *varṇa*. Nor can they be free to pursue their own self-interests as if there were no divinely ordained or transcendent purposes and ends: certainly, the mere pursuit of material wealth and happiness is immoral and wrong. Also, as Juergensmeyer points out: 'The problem that Islam and many other religious traditions have is with the notion of rights: the idea that individuals possess on their own some characteristics that do not come from the community or from God.'[15] For them, what should form the basis of society is virtue and righteousness, not rights.

It is not difficult to see that what we referred to above as the ideology of modernism is the product of the age of Enlightenment and provides the foundation for the liberal conception of social justice. The interesting question that arises, then, is this: If religious nationalism and fundamentalism everywhere, including that within American Protestantism, find modernism and, therefore, liberalism, incompatible with the religious point of view, why don't liberals within Christianity at large (and within Judaism) notice any conflicts? Perhaps they do. But, just in case they do not, it ought to be pointed out that the Enlightenment was as much a protest against Christianity as, perhaps, a product of it. After all, Deism was invented mainly because the Judaeo-Christian view of God and his relationship to the world was seen to be inhospitable to many Enlightenment ideals, including its liberal foundations. It may be recalled that the appeal of Deism was not confined to European intellectuals: some of the founding fathers of America, for example, Thomas Jefferson and Benjamin Franklin, were also deists. When the latter talked of God, therefore, they were not necessarily referring to the God of Christianity. What I am trying to point out is that one does not have to be a fundamentalist to recognize the conflict between Enlightenment liberalism and the demands of traditional religion. If, and to the extent that, Christian and Jewish liberals no longer feel any anguish about that conflict, it may largely be due to the fact that the Enlightenment originated and developed within Christendom; and, after almost three centuries of growing up with Christianity, on the one hand, and liberalism, on the other, they can no longer tell one apart from the other. And when they can separate them and feel the weight of mutual incompatibility, they tend to ease their qualms by taking recourse to two devices, both owing their origins to the Enlightenment. One is the idea of the separation of church and state and the other the separation between the private and the public spheres of an individual's life. The compromise reached, thus, is that one can be Christian (Jewish, and so on) in one's faith, but secular in politics; and, likewise, one can be a servant of God in private life, but a free and sovereign individual in public. Fundamentalism and religious nationalism are disputing whether this twofold separation is either possible or morally right.

Be that as it may, I wish to conclude this chapter by stressing that neither religious nationalism nor fundamentalism is a movement for social justice, in the narrow sense that we have been considering. Quite the contrary, in fact: in their uncompromising rejection of modernism, they also seem to reject one of its products, namely, the liberal and socialist conception of social justice. And I would have to say that, at least on this count, they, rather than, say, Liberation theology, seem to me to be nearer the heart of what religion has been mainly about. Additionally, they, again, rather than Liberation theology, seem to have latched onto the recognition that religion represents, as I shall argue in Chapters 10 and 11, a very different utopia, not just an alternative to, but a foe of, the liberal one.

8 Religion, Politics and Public Life

At least since the founding of the United States of America, the separation of religion and state has been a postulate of modern politics. It is true that this separation has never been complete nor universally maintained, even in the West. Irish politics is notorious for its religious character, and not just in Northern Ireland, although especially so there. In England, the monarch is head of state as well as of the Anglian Church. Italy and Germany, for example, have had Christian Democratic parties which have been dominant powers in the politics of those countries. Even in America, there has seldom in practice existed that 'wall of separation' that Jefferson wanted to see. But, nonetheless, the principle of separation has been largely accepted and practised.

But as we saw in the last chapter, this principle itself is coming increasingly under attack, especially, though not exclusively, in Islamic countries. Iran has been a theocratic state, although with some trappings of a modern democracy, since 1979 and the Sudan turned into one rather recently. The Muslim Brotherhood, and other militant religious groups, are in open warfare with the secular state in Egypt. Practically every major Islamic country is under varying degrees of militant pressure to shed its secular character. Afghanistan, now ruled by a bizarre medley of feuding factions, some fundamentalist, others merely nationalist or tribal, has got rid of a Soviet-backed communist government, but is unable yet to settle the internal feuds. And Algeria barely escaped theocratic rule when its military decided to step into power rather than let the winners of the democratic elections, namely, the religious parties, take the helm of state. But this threat to the separation of religion and state is not confined to Islamic countries.

In India, the Bharatiya Janata Party, an avowedly Hindu religious party, is now the main opposition in parliament, and hoping to become the governing party whenever the next general elections are held. In the case of India, the revival of Hindu nationalism and its declared aim of turning India into a Hindu state derives partly, at least, from the perception, or propaganda, by the BJP and its supporters, that the secular government of India – led largely by the Congress party – has consistently acted against the best interests of the Hindu majority, and for those of the Muslim, and other, minorities. This imbalance needs to be corrected. And the best way of doing so, according to the BJP and its supporters, is to abandon India's secular constitution and make it a Hindu republic; or, at the very least, to interpret secularism in such a way that it does not in practice turn the Hindu majority into an 'oppressed minority'. Partly, at least, then, this is simply 'party-politics', whereby the BJP is exploiting the actual or alleged failures of the Congress and other secular parties. But there clearly is a lot more to it: although sometimes subtly (and at times very crudely) disguised, there is no question that it is, overall, an overt attempt to break down the barriers between religion and state.

The examples so far cited are all of countries where religious parties or sects are overtly trying to undermine existing secular states and replace them with religious ones. And India is especially worth mentioning only because it is a democracy whose constitution can be altered in democratic ways. In America, the other populous democracy, however, there is not yet an overt attempt to turn it into a theocracy, if only because here the power of the constitution remains sacrosanct in the eyes of its people: more than two centuries of constitutional democracy has given it a very firm foundation. But that does not mean that there are not religious interests in America which would like to undermine the foundation: several fundamentalist Christian churches and groups would love to turn America into a 'Christian' state, given half a chance. The fact remains that only the mainstream Protestant churches even concede the principle of the separation of religion and state. The others seem to be merely waiting in the wings to subvert this important foundation of the constitution. The Moral Majority movement was a barely disguised attempt to break down this separation – through the restoration of religious prayer in school, for example. Although this movement was formally suspended a while ago, the Reverend Jerry Falwell keeps threatening to revive it, apparently in response to public demand. The Reverend Pat Robertson's entry into the Republican party primaries as a presidential candidate in 1992 was clearly an effort towards carving a larger niche for religion in the affairs of the state; and his Christian Coalition is not exactly striving to reinforce the wall of separation between church and state. At least some of these religious inroads into American politics were undertaken with the blessings of Ronald Reagan at whose White House, the Reverend Jerry Falwell, and other religious leaders, were honoured guests. Falwell seems to have played a very important role in the re-election of President Reagan who, apparently, called the former an 'instrument of God'.[1]

The question that needs to be asked is: Why is religion everywhere trying to subvert the state, even in countries where their separation is enshrined in a constitution, as, for example, in America and India? In answer, two very general reasons can be put forward. First, some religious people and bodies do not subscribe to the separation of religion and politics, as we saw in the last chapter. According to them, religion not only cannot, but should not, be divorced from the machinery of the state. Islamic fundamentalists, for instance, do not accept that the precepts of the Korān and the *Shariā* are defunct vestiges from the past, and, therefore, incapable of providing solutions to contemporary political and economic problems. On the contrary, it is the separation of politics from 'Islamic values' and laws, inspired and encouraged by the West and Westernized intellectuals, that they see as having eroded the distinctiveness of Islamic culture and heritage and thus given rise to unjust, oppressive and corrupt governments in Islamic countries. Religion, and religious clerics, must, therefore, occupy centre-stage in government and politics again. Such sentiments are echoed not only by the Hindu religious right in India, for example, but also by their Christian counterparts in America and parties of the religious right in Israel. Since these groups do not subscribe to the separation principle, they have no qualms about undermining it by whatever means they can.

But, even supposing, for the sake of the argument, that the separation principle had been acceptable to all religions and to all relevant sections of every religion – a virtually absurd supposition to make – there is little reason to think that, in practice, the separation would have been respected. States and religions have, with rare exceptions, always needed and used each other. The former have tried to win popular support for their policies by appealing to the religious sentiments of people and by seeking the blessings of religious authorities. The latter have tried to acquire legitimacy as the 'official' religion of the country or the region, through the recognition of this status by the state. At heart, attempts in both directions have really been exercises in the pursuit of power. Frequently, and, until recently, practically everywhere, religions have claimed title to both terrestrial and celestial power; and have only reluctantly, if at all, allowed the state to function independently of, and without the blessings of the relevant religion, church or sect. Conversely, traditional monarchs, especially the more powerful among them, had tended to see religion and its proneness to pronouncements on public policy, as a nuisance, at best, and as a threat, at worst; and so, had frequently asserted their divine right to rule, without interference from religious authorities. But, even in modern times, the religious establishment has tried to alter the direction of state policy by acquiring political power – sometimes quite overtly. And politicians – whether aspiring after, or already in, public office, but seeking to win popular support for their policies – have courted religious authorities for

their approval. Politics and religion have always had this ambivalent relationship – each fearing the other's encroachment, on the one hand, but
also, from time to time, needing the other's support. It looks increasingly
the case that religion, especially the religious right, is becoming more
adept in the pursuit of political power and influence. At the same time,
democratic politicians, especially the more opportunistic among them, have
fewer qualms about using whatever means available – including blatant
appeals to religious sentiment – to get elected. Religion and politics, and,
therefore, religion and state, have always, in practice, been hard to keep
apart.

The practical difficulties in separating religion from state notwithstanding, one might still wish to assert that the principle is worth cherishing –
whether or not it is enshrined in the constitution of a country. But as one
considers details of the scope of this separation, one really runs into very
murky waters. For example, since politics is, among other things, a legitimate instrument of the acquisition of power over the machinery of state,
to anyone committed to the principle of separation of religion and state,
politics, in this sense, ought also to be shunned by religion. The former
would seem to entail the latter. But, if so, what precisely does it mean?
Perhaps only that the established churches ought not to engage in this form
of politics. But, then, what of religions which do not have anything resem-
bling an established church? The Bharatiya Janata Party may be a Hindu
political party; but it is in no sense an official representative of Hinduism
as a religion, there being no official Hinduism. And yet it is avowedly
after political power in India. Or, for that matter, in America, the Christian
Coalition does not represent any official church, nor does it claim to be a
political party. But everyone knows that it is after political power. In fact,
it seems to be well known that it has achieved considerable success in this
respect at the local government level, and is now actively engaged in
reshaping the political platform of the Republican party. One could bemoan
this kind of intrusion of religion into power politics, but I doubt that there
is a legitimate way of stopping this. Some might wish to argue that, even
if there were a way, one ought not to try to stop it. It may be worth our
while here to quote a passage from Stephen L. Carter's book, *The Culture
of Disbelief*:

Contemporary American politics faces few greater dilemmas than de-
ciding how to deal with the resurgence of religious belief. On the one
hand, American ideology cherishes religion, as it does all matters of
private conscience, which is why we justly celebrate a strong tradition
against state interference with private religious choice. At the same

time, many political leaders, commentators, scholars and voters are
coming to view any religious element in pubic moral discourse as a tool
of the radical right for reshaping American society. But the effort to
banish religion for politics' sake has led us astray: In our sensible zeal
to keep religion from dominating our politics, we have created a political and legal culture that presses the religiously faithful to be other than
themselves, to act publicly, and sometimes privately as well, as though
their faith does not matter to them.[2]

I will have further comments to make on Carter's position later. For the
moment, I will let the passage above serve as an indication of the kind of
dilemma one faces as soon as one takes the separation principle even to
its closest natural extension in politics – namely, where the objective is the
pursuit of state power – and the organization seeking it is religious but
does not constitute an official church, or its equivalent.

As we move to the loftier – and no longer 'dirty' – sense of politics,
namely, the straightforward activity of democratic participation in the
political process, by a group of concerned citizens who happen to be
religious, there would seem to be no case for keeping religion out of it. On
the contrary, one might argue, that would be highly undesirable indeed.
For it would amount, among other things, to an appeal to keep the legitimate moral role of religion out of politics. And that would be extremely
unfortunate, considering especially that politics already has a bad name,
everywhere, for being indifferent, if not also hostile, to morality. Besides,
as Carter points out, the 'accommodation' of religion and corporate worship into politics, and, therefore, into the affairs of the state, may be
healthier for democracy: for it may be 'closer to Tocqueville's (and the
Founders') conception of religious groups as autonomous moral and political forces, intermediate institutions, separate heads of sovereignty vital
to preventing majoritarian tyranny'.[3] As we move still further towards the
sense of politics in which an individual or a group merely tries to initiate
or influence public policy, where the name politics, if used at all to describe the activity, might as well be an injudicious use of what is merely
participation in public life, the question of separation simply does not
arise. Especially in the case of an individual's participation in public life,
the practical difficulties in keeping the two apart go much deeper. Martin
Marty captures one of these in the following words:

We must begin with a given. Religion is much involved with public life.
Even the attempts to disengage the two spheres involves one with both.
For the United States Supreme Court to argue that civil government
must have nothing to do with religion demands an argument not only

about civility but also about religion. Citizens for the most part 'belong' to religious and public realms and cannot completely chop their lives in two.[4]

I may, for example, be a strong libertarian in my political outlook which makes me work towards ensuring that people enjoy the freedom of choice in all matters that affect their lives. But if I happen to be a committed Catholic at the same time, and, therefore, oppose abortion, I might wish to deny a woman's right to choose. Given this unfortunate conflict, I would, at the very least, be obliged to search for a framework which either eliminates this conflict or allows me to find an honourable compromise. Whether or not I like it, my politics (in practically all senses of the word) and my religion seem to be on a 'collision' course, and I have to do something about it.

What applies to people, individually, does so to religious bodies too – and in a similar way. The Catholic church, for example, may concede that it ought to stay out of politics. But that may not prevent the Catholic bishops from writing to the White House, for example, that Hillary Clinton's Task Force on Health-Care reform in America must not provide for a woman's right to free abortion at the expense of the taxpayer. Likewise, the Society of Friends, the organization of Quakers, while professing the separation of church and state, may, at the same time, feel no hesitation in defending the right of the conscientious objector not to be drafted by the state into military service. Examples of this sort can be cited almost endlessly; but it should be unnecessary to add to those given above. Just as the various realms – the political, the religious and the moral, to name just a few – cannot be neatly separated in the case of individuals, so are they difficult to keep apart in the case of voluntary groups. And religious bodies, for the most part, are voluntary associations of human beings. The moral obligations and outlooks of human beings – whether as individuals or as members of an association – are shaped just as much by political idealism as by religious commitment, if not more so. Sometimes the two may complement each other; at other times, they may be in conflict. And while the way one comes to terms with the conflict may vary from one individual to another, or one group to another, each of the responses will still provide testimony to the mutual involvement of religion on the one hand, and state, politics, and public affairs on the other.

These are some of the practical problems involved in keeping religion and state (or politics, generally) apart. It is important at this point to notice a moral dilemma – ambivalence, at the very least – that even committed proponents of separation might encounter. We do often expect our churches or other religious bodies to speak out against state-sponsored tyranny, oppression or injustice, whatever the cost to them of such pronouncements. The silence of the official churches during the Nazi pogrom, even while individuals – lay persons or clerics – voiced their opposition to the persecution of the Jews, has ever since the Second World War been held as a major failure of the religious establishment. Yet, logically, if religion ought not to meddle in matters of state, then what the churches were doing was the right thing. This ambivalence arises from the fact that every religious tradition offers shining examples of the 'prophetic voice' or the 'wisdom of the sage' or the 'courage of the incorruptible', capable of occupying a superior moral vantage point and declaring, 'This can't go on, because it is immoral, evil or against God's laws, etc!' This is what I take Carter to mean when he refers to religion as the voice of resistance.[5] Recognition of this fact, – namely, that religion may possibly be the source of a superior morality or wisdom which places it in a position sometimes to say that the laws given by the state can, and should, be disobeyed – creates a structural problem in enforcing the separation principle. I call it a 'structural' problem, because, in a way, it invites religion to pronounce on matters of state, of public morality and of justice and injustice, even while conceding, (when it is conceding) the principle of the separation of the two spheres.

It seems to me that these difficulties discussed in the preceding paragraphs require a careful analysis of the grounds for advocating the principle of separation. Before looking at some of these grounds, it may be useful to mention that there is no inconsistency in enumerating all the actual – practical and structural – difficulties in enforcing the separation of religion and state, while simultaneously maintaining that, nonetheless, they *ought* to remain separate. Some may even wish to argue – and they may or may not be purists – that the real test of our moral commitment only comes when the obstacles in accomplishing it are formidable. Be that as it may, an examination of the grounds for the principle of separation between religion and state would seem by now to be overdue.

The most classic statement of separation between religion and state – certainly the best known – is this statement attributed to Jesus: 'Pay the emperor what belongs to the emperor, and pay God what belongs to God.'[6] Because of its cryptic character and of the circumstances in which it was made, it has naturally been subject to somewhat varying interpretations. But, nonetheless, it is difficult to doubt that, if it meant anything at all, it did, at least, imply a warning against mixing religion with state, the transcendent with the terrestrial, the divine with the worldly, the sacred with the profane.

The rationale for the separation can be expressed in two different but related ways. The state and religion have different functions, methods and purposes. The first is about securing specifiable goals, of a political, economic or legal character, designed to secure order or justice in this world, or specific parts of it. Such order may be established through conquest, as was the case almost universally until relatively recently, or through revolution as in eighteenth-century France or America, or through the expression of citizen's wishes as in contemporary democratic societies. Religion, on the other hand, is primarily about transcendental goals, supernatural objectives, or about dreams of a heavenly realm. Establishing order is not part of this dream, because that is already presupposed. The methods appropriate to the attainment of this realm do not, and cannot, include either conquest, revolution or popular consent. The way to this kingdom or realm lies in self-surrender, in *agape*, divine love, the conquest of the ego, or the attainment of emancipating wisdom. The two, therefore, are not to be confused, although, as a matter of fact, they often will be confused, given our own limitations as humans and of the world we inhabit.

The other way in which this separation can be spoken of is by emphasizing the dichotomy between the external and the internal, the public and the private, or between the 'shadow' and the 'substance', using Platonic terms. Religion is concerned with the second half of each of these pairs, and the state with the first. Progress in the two realms is, and should be, judged by entirely different criteria: success or failure in achieving power, peace, justice, happiness, consensus and so on, in the former; harmony between one's self and the ultimate reality, submission to the will of God, cultivation of a pervasive internal state of love and joy, compassion or detachment, or the mystic absorption into 'the other', and so on, in the case of the latter. The language chosen to describe the purposes of the two spheres may almost appear to make the case of separation self-evident, so much so that anyone failing to consent to the principle of separation may be considered guilty of obtuseness. Yet, since a single individual may be both a political citizen and a religious believer, there will be problems in keeping the two apart. But, nevertheless, it can be plausibly said, the two *should* be kept apart; and even, that, ultimately, the former does not matter.

If this argument in philosophical/conceptual terms fails to convince the sceptic, however, a pragmatic argument is easily constructed, citing the dangers of not keeping the power of state out of the reach of religion or *vice versa*. History is replete with episodes of the tyranny unleashed by a dominant religion on those who dared to disagree regarding what to believe. One may recall the horrors of the Crusades and the *Jihads*; the centuries of persecution of the Jews, or of any other religious minority by the dominant religion of a country or region. It was this background of religious persecution that sent the persecuted flocking across the Atlantic to what came to be the United States of America. And this persecution, although engineered by the dominant religion, church or sect, was perpetrated with the aid – at least, the blessing – of the state authorities. Certainly, the European states concerned did nothing to stop the practice. It was the deep and painful awareness of this fact, among others, on the part of the founding fathers of America – rather than merely abstract reasoning – that, I think, made them legislate the constitutional separation of religion and state. Madison's language of the first clause of his original fourth amendment in the Bill of Rights sums up very clearly the intended spirit of what came to be known as the 'establishment clause'. 'The civil rights of none shall be abridged on account of religious belief or worship, nor shall any national religion be established, nor shall the full and equal rights of conscience be in any manner, or any pretext, infringed.'[7] The freedom and dignity of every individual – irrespective of religious belief, so far only a philosopher's dream – had at last been given a constitutional foundation.

Certainly before this constitutional grounding of the separation of church and state, and, to some extent, even after this event, the many churches in America had frequently made concerted efforts to establish their denomination as the official religion of the country – or at least of the state in which they were dominant. The founding fathers, however, were determined to preserve the pluralistic character of American society in the face of these sectarian inroads. And anyone who cares to think deeply about this accomplishment of the founders cannot but help noticing how farsighted it was. For religious pluralism in America two hundred odd years ago was a pale shadow of what it is today. In those days, apart from a slowly growing but still insignificant minority of Jews, the churches and denominations were all Christian. Today, however, America has sizeable populations not only of Jews but also of Muslims, Hindus, Buddhists, Bahais and a lot more, not to mention a religiously distinct population of native Americans who in those days were simply not considered. If preserving the distinctiveness of all religious groups, so that they could live their own ways of life without fear of persecution, mattered then, it clearly matters immensely more so now. The strife resulting from any attempt to declare America a Christian country – as some in America would like to do – could be mind-numbing, even to contemplate as a remote possibility. But the separation principle does not derive its vindication from this fear alone. There is the larger, and nobler, insight that religious pluralism is a good thing intrinsically, arising from the thinking that no one religion could claim an exclusive access to 'transcendental truth', whatever that might be; and so the more perspectives open to us there are, the better off we are as humans, collectively. This respect for pluralism can itself provide a very sound defence of the separation principle. My defence of religious pluralism may appear questionable to some; and I am not unaware of the philosophical difficulties involved in taking that position. But this is not, in my opinion, the appropriate place for a detailed analysis of the issues involved. Besides, I have tried to do it elsewhere.[8]

But pluralism is not the only potential victim of the failure of the separation principle. Some may wish to argue that when religion assumes or becomes part of the power structure of the state, it almost inevitably leads to the emergence of the psychological spirit of conformity among its people, instead of innovation and free thought. Slowly but surely, it is not just other behaviour that becomes regulated, but limits are placed even on what can be thought and said. Those wondering why, need only look back to what Bruno, Copernicus, Galileo, Descartes and Kant had to put up with by way of state obstruction to their free thought and speech. And today one need look no farther than Iran to discover the straitjacket of conformity in dress, speech, thought and behaviour that its people have to fit into. This is not just the loss of pluralism, although that loss is big enough: this entails the loss of individual autonomy as a human being, who ceases to be an end in himself/herself and becomes a mere tool in the enactment of some externally imposed blueprint of how the world ought to be. Those who want to reject this imputation of adolescence to humanity at large would wish to do everything possible to avert the imposition of authoritarian power by religion, as, indeed, from any other source. And if the separation of religion and state is a means to avoiding that ominous future, then one must insist on it, just as the founding fathers of America did two centuries ago.

But the mixing of religion and politics, of the spiritual quest with the pursuit of state power is not just bad for the state and for its citizens. It does not just distort the nature of politics and of debate about public affairs. It is bad for religion itself. As is well known, power corrupts; and a church or religion in pursuit of political power soon loses hold of its higher calling. Too much preoccupation with the terrestrial dims the light of the celestial message. Anyone familiar with even the broad outlines of world history, will be able to recall a few episodes of the corruption of the guardians of religion when they roamed too freely in the corridors of power. By all accounts, the Brahmins of India enjoyed and commanded their moral authority, almost divine status, only when they served as all-sacrificing, wise sages, to whom worldly wealth or power meant nothing.

But as the caste system solidified into a hereditary system, and the number of Brahmins grew; and as they became more and more involved in becoming 'king-makers' and wielders of political authority, without the wisdom to command it, it became increasingly difficult to tell them apart from anyone else. The spiritual quest and the sacrifice of material possessions entailed by that quest meant very little to the bulk of Brahmins. As they thus lost their capacity for spiritual leadership, Hinduism gradually fossilized as a religion, to be revived only occasionally during the last several centuries, often by poets and mystics and devotees who were mostly non-Brahmins. The Brahmins might possibly have been the first victims of the corrosive effects of political power: they certainly were not the last. Those who have read about the lust for power, political intrigues and the extravagant and debauched lifestyles of some of the popes who ruled during the Middle Ages, will have no difficulty seeing how far away from the message of Jesus Christ they had deviated. Similar unease is caused by the hedonistic and corrupt lifestyles of some of the contemporary 'televangelists' in America and the almost naked pursuit of political power by others on the religious right.

The consequences of such corruption are far-reaching: people, instead of being inspired, are put off by religion. When Brahmins and popes, priests and clergy cannot be distinguished easily through their preoccupation with transcendental purposes, people naturally drift into thinking that religion has nothing unique to offer. And this leads not only to the distrust of religion, but also to disenchantment with it. I think it should be clear that I favour the separation of church and state, and of religion and politics, when politics is understood as the pursuit of state power, despite all the practical and structural difficulties such separation involves. The separation clause in the Constitution leaves no doubt in our minds, for instance, that the state must not establish any religion: this is not, and cannot be, one of the state's legitimate roles. It is equally clear that the state must not in any way 'abridge' or curtail the fundamental civil rights of any individual on account of his/her religious views or practices. On the other hand, religion must not be given the right to form a militia or the authority to levy taxes. When any of those limits might in practice have been crossed is frequently difficult to judge; but doubts about these are ultimately resolved through an appeal to the courts. Not everyone is, or need be, satisfied by what the courts decide in a given case; but the constitutional judicial process is available and open to every individual or group.

Talking of the courts, I ought to point out that, according to Carter, the American judicial system has been wrong in interpreting the separation clause as implying the exercise of neutrality by the state, that is, being neither for nor against religion. He thinks that this doctrine of neutrality should be replaced by that of 'accommodation'. While I am not competent to offer an opinion on this matter when it is presented as a problem in jurisprudence, I have, earlier in this chapter, taken a sympathetic view of this accommodation principle, understood at the level of common-sense. For, among other things, this principle requires that people's religious views should be taken seriously, and does not lead to the demand to forbid 'statements of religious belief in the course of public dialogue'.[9] It acknowledges that people's religious beliefs do matter to them; and, by implication, fully expects them to bring these beliefs into discussions of public policy. My defence of the separation of religion and state and of religion and politics – in the precise context in which I defend the latter – certainly should not demand what Carter calls the 'separation of faith and self',[10] namely, the demand or expectation that people keep their faith out of any debate about public policy. Indeed, that, I think, would be very unfortunate, for reasons given earlier.

Equally unfortunate, however, would be to let faith, or what sometimes goes under that name, serve as a fortress shielding one from the requirements of rational debate about public policy. I must be free to bring my views on public policy into debate, whatever might be the source of these views; but, equally, I must not expect them automatically to become the last word in the debate, simply because they have a religious source. Nor must I be seen to be ever ready to clothe all my mundane concerns into the garb of the sacred. That is another kind of trivialization of faith, this time brought about by the believer himself or herself. The believer's proneness to 'sacralize politics', to use the phrase employed by Cardinal Ratzinger in castigating Liberation theology, does nothing to enhance one's estimation of the integrity of faith, or add to the quality or clarity of the debate about public policy. Religion in public life may well be 'a sign of the unlimited in the limited world of public policy',[11] as Marty very suggestively puts it. But religion, and only religion, deals with 'the unlimited'. We have a host of other means for dealing with 'the limited': we call them politics, economics, biology, ecology, medicine, law and engineering, as the case may be.

9 The Kingdom of God and the 'Good Life' on Earth

As we saw in Chapter 3, all the great religions seem to entertain a highly significant notion of an ideal society, referred to variously as *Rāma-Rājya*, *Sukhāvatī*, or the kingdom of God. The precise meaning of these (and other related concepts, for example, heaven) varies between religions and, even within a religious tradition, is interpreted somewhat differently by various sects, churches and theologians. But I think that there is sufficient resemblance among the concepts for us to be able to specify a few general features, without being bogged down, I hope, in abstruse theological controversy or culture-specific historical detail.

One of these general observations, it seems to me, is that the kingdom, reign or realm spoken of has, contrary to appearances, a transcendental reference. It is sometimes identified as a coming into being again of something that has already existed in the past. The dream of *Rāma-Rājya*, for example, is a wish for the re-establishment in future of a state or society which already existed when Rama, the reincarnation of Vishnu, ruled in the 'historical' past. Similarly, the kingdom of God that is to usher in the era of joy and righteousness and peace in the future – whether spoken of by Jews, Christians or Muslims – is, in a sense, to be a partial re-enactment of the rule of David, or the rule of Yahweh, which had been in existence in the historical past. 'Formerly the kingship was vested in Israel, but when they sinned it was taken from them and given to the other nations. . . . But tomorrow when Israel repents, God will take it from the idolaters and the kingship shall be to the Lord.'[1] Similarly, the Golden Age, *Satya yuga*, that Hinduism speaks of as the first of the four great ages or epochs, when truth and righteousness reigned, will once again return when the present evil age, *Kali yuga*, is destroyed and a new phase in the cyclic order of creation and destruction is inaugurated.

What is worth noting, however, is that this ideal kingdom is never, or seldom, spoken of as existing in the present, although both Hebrew and Christian sources occasionally appear to do so. Jesus, to be sure, gives the impression from time to time that the kingdom of God might have been ushered in already and that he and his disciples were to be the witnesses to this great event. But, according to the Synoptic Gospels, he sees it as, at best, the beginning of the unfolding of the kingdom, and not as something that was already there in finished form. He would not, otherwise, ask his disciples to pray for it,[2] or say 'Thou art not far from the Kingdom of God',[3] and clearly not assert that it would come within a generation.[4] Consequently, for Jesus, the coming of the kingdom is a future happening, overall, and not a present fact. After examining a number of passages from the Synoptic Gospels relating to the kingdom of God, James Price concludes:

> when Jesus spoke of the kingdom of God as 'coming' he spoke of an eschatological hope. It is true that in ancient Judaism the phrase *kingdom of God* could refer to a present reality perceived by faith: God rules His World; He always has and He always will. It was possible to speak of this everlasting kingdom as an established reality whenever and wherever God's people acknowledged His supremacy and obey his will. But it is unlikely that any of the passages above can be properly understood in this way. In proclaiming the 'coming' of the kingdom of God, Jesus testified to his generation that God would usher in that new Age to which the prophets and writers of apocalypse had looked forward. This day of judgment and of salvation was 'at hand'.[5]

Similarly, even in the tradition of the Old Testament, 'Deutero-Isaiah understands the reality of this [kingdom] as still in the future, and announces it as imminent.'[6] And 'Later writers [of the Hebrew Religion], whose concepts are already preparing the way for the apocalyptic, reach out further in their expectation.'[7]

This feature, namely, that the kingdom is either a past event or a future possibility, but never really, on the whole, a present experience, implies, in my opinion, that it is best viewed as a transcendent state, despite the use of phrases that give it the appearance of a historical or pseudo-historical occurrence. In a sense, of course, no future can be completely unconnected to the present: any talk of the future logically entails a contrast with the present and the past. But it is significant that the kingdom does not refer to a present state of society or government. Wolfhart Pannenberg's interpretation deserves special notice here:

> Jesus proclaimed the rule of God as a reality belonging to the future. This is the coming kingdom. The idea was not new, being a conventional aspect of Jewish expectation. What was new was Jesus' understanding that God's claim on the world is to be viewed exclusively in terms of his coming rule. Thus it is necessary to say that, in a restricted but important sense, God does not yet exist. Since his rule and his being are inseparable, God's being is still in the process of coming to be. Considering this, God should not be mistaken for an objectified being

presently existing in its fullness. In this light, the current criticism directed against the traditional theistic idea of God is quite right. Obviously, if the mode of God's being is interlocked with the coming of his rule, we should not be surprised or embarrassed that God cannot be 'found' somewhere in present reality.[8]

It would seem that, unlike Nietzsche, Pannenberg cannot declare God to be dead, for he is scarcely born yet! Be that as it may, though, his understanding of the kingdom of God lends weight to the opinions of those who have maintained that it is not of this world, and, therefore, is not to be identified with some earthly regime or social order.

Lest there be any lingering doubts that this kingdom may after all have something to do with this world, we need only look at the polar opposition St Augustine sees between the City of God and the 'earthly city', the former the 'society of the redeemed' and the latter the 'society of the devil'.

Accordingly, two cities have been formed by two loves: the earthly by the love of self, even to the contempt of God; the heavenly by the love of God, even to the contempt of self. The former, in a word, glories in itself, the latter in the Lord. For the one seeks glory from men, but the greatest glory of the other is God, the Witness of Conscience. The one lifts up its head, in its own glory; the other says to its God, 'Thou art my glory, and the lifter of mine head.'[9]

Although the church on this earth may, according to him, be something of a refuge from the world, even it is not what the kingdom to come will be. And a similar contrast is drawn by Martin Luther between the kingdom of God and the 'kingdom of the world'.

All who are not Christians belong to the kingdom of the world and are under the law. Since few believe and still fewer live a Christian life, do not resist the evil, and themselves do no evil, God has provided for non-Christians a different government outside the Christian estate and God's kingdom, and has subjected them to the sword, so that, even though they would do so, they cannot practice their wickedness, and that, if they do, they may not do it without fear nor in peace and prosperity.[10]

Similarly, Calvin says, 'But he who knows how to distinguish between the body and the soul, between his present transitory life and the future eternal one, will find no difficulty in understanding that the spiritual kingdom of Christ and civil government are things very different and remote from each other.'[11] If one were to follow the line of reasoning of these Christian luminaries, such as Augustine, Luther, Calvin etc., it would seem that, while injustices and inequalities in this world may be alleviated somewhat through human effort, springing out of love or compassion, true justice can only be found in the kingdom of God.

And this conclusion may not be a minor corollary, but a fact of the highest importance, since what is required as a necessary condition for the establishment of God's kingdom is not a little tampering with existing laws, practices or hierarchies, but a radical transformation of human nature. For the citizens of this kingdom-to-be would be only the 'remnants' or 'kernels', those who have been redeemed after the judgment. The Hebrew tradition views the kingdom as ruled by justice and righteousness. It is also characterized by peace and joy; and, speaking negatively, where the redeemed shall not sorrow anymore.[12] It is this spiritual transformation that also receives the most emphasis in the New Testament. The kingdom is the realm of righteousness, of justice and of peace and joy, but, above all, of love. Freed from sin, its subjects live in utter, loving submission to the will of God and in a state of abiding love with each other. This spiritual and moral metamorphosis of humanity seemed to many Enlightenment thinkers – perhaps, above all, to Kant – to be so central to the New Testament idea of the kingdom of God, that they, forgetting history and scripture, to some extent, started seeing the kingdom as referring to an internal state: 'the kingdom of God is within you'.[13] It was this process of making biblical ideas fit Enlightenment rational ideas and ideals, I think, that tended for a time to underplay the transcendental conception of the kingdom of God. Most modern theologians, however, recognize the full importance of the eschatological element in the sayings of Jesus, and are, to that extent, less likely to see the kingdom as referring merely to an internal state of enlightenment.

In Hinduism and Buddhism, however, the corresponding ideas of the kingdom are much more likely to be interpreted as a state of wisdom (*jnāna*). For here the human malaise is not wilfulness and sin primarily, but the state of individual and cosmic ignorance (*avidyā*) and the consequent attachment to the inessential. So even when the 'kingdom' – whether it is *Rāma-Rājya*, the 'Golden Age', or *Sukhāvatī* – is spoken of as a historical or mythic-historic event, it is not very difficult to make the case that such descriptions are metaphorical or allegorical references to the internal state of an individual's moral and spiritual enlightenment. Since this characteristic of the religious quest in Eastern, especially Indian, religions is so well known, it should be unnecessary to elaborate on it any further here. What does need mention, however, is that the Hindu idea of the 'ages' of the world contains the notion that, as the world progresses, or rather regresses, from the first to the fourth age, there is a 'progressive decline in piety, morality, strength, stature, longevity and happiness'.[14] Indeed, according to one interpretation, there may even be an eschatological element, especially in the notion of *Kali yuga*, the last of the four ages of the world. The decline through the ages is symbolically represented as a bull, signifying *dharma*, which has four legs in the first age – when truth and righteousness prevail – but is left with only one by the time *Kali yuga*, the age of falsehood and impiety, arrives. Interestingly, there seems to me a strong parallel between the Hindu idea of *Kali yuga*, the end of which restores the 'Golden Age' again, and the idea of the apocalyptic in Israelite religion. Here is a description of the latter given by Helmer Ringgren:

> The present age is in the power of evil and sin; it culminates in a furious assault of the forces of evil. Towards the end, the sufferings of the righteous are intensified to the limit. They are often described as 'birth pangs' or the 'messianic woes', since they precede the appearance of the Messiah. . . . There follows . . . the intervention of God, the day of the Lord, the Great Judgment. God conquers the enemy and judges the evil ones. The righteous are set free and enter the new world, the kingdom of God. The new eon has come.[15]

This narrative would be hard to improve on as a depiction of the circumstances heralding the incarnation on earth of the Hindu God, Vishnu, and the beginning of, say, the reign of Rama, *Rāma-Rājya*. Truth and righteousness are also the hallmarks of *Rāma-Rājya*. According to Gandhi, 'Rama did justice even to a dog. By abandoning his kingdom and living in the forest for the sake of truth, Rama gave to all the kings of the world an object-lesson in noble conduct.'[16] *Rāma-Rājya*, like the kingdom of God, may be a social utopia, but it is so only because in it truth, righteousness, nobility of character – moral uprightness, in other words, and religious piety and wisdom – are the essential attributes of the ruler and the ruled.

To what extent is the kingdom of God a hedonist's paradise? This question needs to be asked because, if it is, after all, a land of milk and honey and all the other material goods in plenty (*and not much else*), then at least the better-off citizens of the affluent parts of the world today may well feel that they need be in no hurry to get there, for they have it all here already. And there is no gainsaying the fact that, frequently, this kingdom is identified with heaven or paradise wherein every entrant is guaranteed eternal life, peace, joy and happiness. They suffer no pain and have all the pleasures at their command. It is not altogether incidental that America, soon to be the land of matchless material prosperity, was regarded by many millenarian religious figures as the country where God's kingdom was in the process of being established. And at least some of them foresaw the material progress of America as a natural concomitant of the coming of the kingdom. Richard Niebuhr quotes from one such visionary, namely, Samuel Hopkins, who prophesied that the coming of the kingdom, while it will be 'a time of universal peace, love, and general and cordial friendship', will also, simultaneously, be a 'time of great enjoyment, happiness and universal joy', not only:

> for spiritual but also for material reasons. Natural calamities will be prevented by divine providence; war with its impoverishment of men will have been abolished; intemperance and excess will be discarded; . . . there will be 'great improvement in the mechanic arts by which the earth will be subdued and cultivated, and all the necessary and convenient articles of life, such as utensils, clothing, building, etc. will be formed and made in a better manner, and with much less labor than they now are.[17]

Had Hopkins been alive today, he would almost certainly have thought this part of his prophecy to have been dramatically vindicated! But whether he would have agreed that America today was indeed God's kingdom come, in moral and spiritual ways, is another matter.

Not only in the biblical religions, however, is the kingdom associated with material wealth and grandeur. Among Mahāyāna Buddhist texts, *The Larger Sukhāvatī-Vyūha*, for example, sees no need any longer for the Bodhisattvas in *Sukhāvatī* to have to perform the mundane tasks of 'dyeing, sewing, drying and washing' of their cloaks, for they will now be 'covered by newly produced excellent cloaks, granted to them by the *Tathāgata*'; they would be 'free from pain'; they would, in that Buddha country, be able to get 'from different jewel-trees . . . a mass of excellent ornaments'; and will not there 'suffer any diminution in the strength of their senses';[18] and no being in that Buddha country can possibly help exclaiming 'That Buddha country possesses so much beauty and so much magnificence'![19] It also describes an immense Bodhi-tree, extending hundreds of miles in every direction, covered with 'many hundred thousand colours, of different leaves, of different flowers, of different fruits, adorned with many beautiful ornaments . . . in fact, adorned according to the desires of beings whatever their wishes may be'; and of such extraordinary powers that 'for those beings whose hearing [the sound of] that Bodhi-tree reaches, no disease of the ear is to be feared until they reach Bodhi (highest knowledge)'; and, likewise, no diseases of the eye for those who see this tree and no diseases of the nose for those receiving its smell',[20] and so on.

What the last two paragraphs have tried to show is that there is clearly some basis in text and tradition for the impression that, at least as a secondary effect, material well-being and happiness might accompany the coming of the kingdom. But anyone tempted to think that this concept is primarily, or even importantly, about the creation of a hedonist paradise on earth, is, in my opinion, grossly in error, not only in the understanding of this concept, but even of religion itself. For religion, almost by definition, cannot be primarily about this world, nor about wealth, or even a just distribution of wealth in it. Its focus has to remain transcendental, spiritual and moral; and given this focus, material goods or happiness would not only fade into insignificance but may, in all likelihood, be seen as hindrances to the properly religious quest. 'It is easier for a camel to go through the eye of a needle than for a rich man to enter the kingdom of God',[21] sets the tone for the understanding of the place of wealth in the pursuit of the kingdom. And the equally famous beatitude, 'Blessed are you poor, for yours is the Kingdom of God',[22] powerfully reinforces it. Augustine explains the true rationale for sacrifice – not just the abandoning of craving for things merely material, but the spirit of sacrifice in every act that a true seeker of the heavenly city must cultivate:

There is, then, a true sacrifice in every work which unites us in a holy communion with God, that is, in every work that is aimed at that final Good in which alone we can be truly blessed. . . . For this reason, a man himself who is consecrated in the name of God and vowed to God is a sacrifice, inasmuch as he dies to the world that he may live for God. For this is a part of that mercy which each one has on himself, according to the text: 'Have pity on thy own soul, pleasing God'. . . . Our body, too, is a sacrifice when, for God's sake, we chasten it, as we ought, by temperance, that is when we do not yield our members as 'instruments of iniquity unto sin', but as means of holiness to God. The Apostle exhorts us to this when he says: 'I exhort you, therefore, brethren, by the mercy of God to present your bodies as a sacrifice, living, holy, pleasing to God – your spiritual service.' If, then, the body, which is less than the soul and which the soul uses as a servant or a tool, is a sacrifice when it is used well and rightly for the service of God, how much more so is the soul when it offers itself to God so that, aflame in the fire of divine Love, and with the dross of worldly desire melted away, it is remolded into the unchangeable form of God and becomes beautiful in his sight by reason of the bounty of beauty which he has bestowed upon it. This is what the Apostle implies in the following verse: 'And be not conformed to this world, but be transformed in the newness of your mind, that you may discern what is the good and acceptable and perfect will of God.'[23]

I have thought it fit to reproduce this lengthy extract from Augustine, partly because I have wondered whether many in the West, especially the so-called 'social activists' among them, are even aware of traditional Christianity's message of 'dying to the world' and of the 'dross of worldly desire melting away', spoken of above. To them, these phrases may be more reminiscent of what they would regard as the 'world-and-life-denying' religions of the East. In this latter impression, they are not at all wrong, as I will proceed to show immediately. The same *Sukhāvatī-Vyūha*, which was quoted earlier as portraying *Sukhāvatī* as the land of 'jewel-trees' and 'ornaments', 'free from pain', and so on, has quite a different message as we approach the end of the text. Fairly early on, it talks of the 'incomparable happiness of Nirvana', but goes on to add: 'and this also I shall explain as vain'.[24] Then, reminiscent of phrases just quoted from Augustine it avows that beings born in this country (that is, *Sukhāvatī*) will not 'form any idea of property, even with regard to their body'.[25] This is repeated in verse 38 which goes on to add the following, pertaining to the true character of 'this land' and its inhabitants:

> [They] feel neither pleasure nor pain; stepping forward they have no desire . . . ; for those beings who have been born in that world, . . . there is no idea of others, no idea of self, no idea of inequality, no strife, no dispute, no opposition. Full of equanimity, of benevolent thought, of tender thought, of serene thought, of firm thought, of unbiased thought, of undisturbed thought, of unagitated thought, of thought (fixed on) the practice of discipline and transcendent wisdom, having entered on knowledge which is a firm support to all thoughts, equal to the ocean in wisdom, equal to the mountain Meru in knowledge, rich in many good qualities, delighting in the music of the Bodhyangas, devoted to the music of Buddha, they discard the eye of flesh, and assume the heavenly eye. And having approached the eye of wisdom, having reached the eye of the Law, producing the eye of Buddha, showing it, lighting it, and fully exhibiting it, they attain perfect wisdom. . . .[26]

It may be instructive here to quote a few passages from Aquinas in order to show that it is not only Augustine, among the great Christian thinkers, who shares the 'other-worldliness' preached by Eastern religions. Aquinas, having already declared that human happiness does not consist in the goods of the body,[27] goes on to say:

> Man's ultimate happiness consists in the contemplation of truth for this operation is specific to man and is shared with no other animals. Also it is not directed to any other end since the contemplation of truth is

sought for its own sake. In addition, in this operation man is united to higher beings (substances) since this is the only human operation that is carried out both by God and by the separate substances (*angels*). Through this operation too man is united with those higher beings by knowing them in a certain way.[28]

He goes on to affirm that man's ultimate happiness is not in this life: 'No one therefore is happy in this life.'[29]

Because of the close connections between Buddhist and Hindu conceptualizations of the highest good, it should not be necessary to argue that the latter would require the life of physical bliss – whether in heaven or *Rāma-Rājya*, to be sacrificed, transcended, if one were to reach the highest state envisioned by Hinduism, namely, *mokṣa*, what the *Sukhāvatī-Vyūha*, just quoted, called 'perfect wisdom'. What may need arguing, however, is that even Islam is no stranger to such sentiments. According to Shirazi (Mulla Sadra), one of the most influential Islamic thinkers:

> Therefore you must completely free the Heart (from any attachments to the body) and totally purify the innermost self. You must be rigorously detached from created being, and (devote yourself to) repeated intimate communion with the Truly Real, in spiritual retreat. And you must shun the carnal desires, the various forms of the will to dominate, and the other animal ends (which follow from our bodily condition), by means of a pure and untroubled inner intention and sincere faith. In this way your action will itself become your reward. And your knowledge will be precisely the same as your attaining the Goal of your aspiration, so that when *the dark covering is removed* (50:22) and the veil is lifted (from your heart and inner vision), you will be standing in the Presence of the Lord of Lords – just as you already were in your *innermost heart* (2:269: etc.).[30]

Any attempt to bring out the true significance of the kingdom of God, and its cognate concepts in Eastern religions, is important in its own right. They encapsulate some of the ideals nurtured by these religions, whose precise meaning and content needs to be understood, especially, since, as I have hinted earlier, there are grounds for thinking that misunderstandings exist in this respect. The particular misunderstanding that concerns me here is the supposition made that this notion, that is, of the kingdom of God, entails the political obligation to create a just society on this earth, especially in its distributive sense. While any sensible person would, and should, welcome any excuse for the creation of a just society here – for justice can hardly be said to be abundant on earth, in any of its senses –

it ought to be pointed out in the interests of accuracy that the idea of the kingdom cannot legitimately be said to entail that. It certainly does not appear to be its primary message, although it has to be confessed that there is some ambiguity there, since, as we saw earlier, there are clear indications that material prosperity and happiness may be the incidental rewards going with the citizenship of the kingdom. Also, there is the fairly common interpretation put on the idea of the kingdom, primarily in the West, but not lacking elsewhere either, that although the kingdom can only be established by God, we can help prepare for it through our 'good works'. Since this interpretation is part of the tradition, I cannot say that it is fanciful or wrong. But it seems to me that when full account is taken of the primarily spiritual and moral message of the kingdom and of its transcendental reference, as I have argued earlier, it becomes less plausible, on the whole, to maintain that economic and political justice on earth – especially if this is taken to be identical with some secular notion of social justice – can be a primary goal of religion. Incidentally, if it strikes anyone as odd or capricious that I should equate the notion of *Sukhāvatī* with the kingdom of God, when Buddhism is, in fact, non-theistic, I would like to remind them that the Buddha is occasionally referred to as the 'king of kings'.[31]

In any case, my main reason for emphasizing the spiritual and moral content of the idea of the kingdom is to highlight how a proper recognition of this may, even at this late stage in our history, help bring us back from the brink of possible disaster. I am referring to the fact that the secular, modern, hedonistic conception of the 'good life' and the consumerism that it generates, has, over the centuries, created immense environmental and ecological dangers for the world we live in. If the world's population continues to expand, as it has done in the past, and if, at the same time, our per capita rate of consumption across the world keeps increasing, as seems to be the case as well, then by all credible accounts, life on earth may become impossible in the not-too-distant future. At the very least, the 'quality of life' may suffer irreparable harm through the net effects of pollution, deforestation, the destruction of the ozone layer, the possible melting of the polar ice-caps, and other similar dreaded possibilities. Such talk has become so commonplace these days that many otherwise sensible people may even have become 'desensitized' to it, regarding it as the neurotic, or even lunatic, outbursts of the 'prophets of doom and gloom'. So why am I raising this subject at all? The answer is that this alleged looming environmental nightmare, even if its scope is enormously exaggerated, should not have been our desert today, if the 'desirelessness' and 'dying to this world' preached by our religions – and discussed above –

had been heeded by our ancestors – immediate as well as remote – not to mention our contemporaries. So what happened? How did we get to this state of affairs?

Obviously a great deal will need to be said in answer, certainly much more than I am competent to, or have time here to say. But, I think the finger of suspicion must be raised in the direction, among others, of the failure of religion either to grasp the lesson properly, or else to teach it effectively. In fact, it must be a bit of both, it seems to me. Since no part of the world has managed to escape the evils of environmental and ecological degradation, all our major religions must share the guilt of failure, but perhaps not all in equal measure. Christianity's culpability must, it seems to me, be far greater, for the simple reason that it has been the religion of the ruling powers for the best part of the last 500 years, which is the period when capitalism, consumerism and the 'conquest of nature' have flourished. As the religion of the imperial powers, it, at least in principle, had the ability to resist and fight the forces responsible for the current mess. After all, which among these powers gave any thought to what Hinduism, Buddhism, or Islam had to say, on anything? It has been argued that our environmental ills owe a great deal to the wrong model of our relationship to nature preached by the biblical religions. Whatever the merits of that contention, I do not intend to discuss it here, because it has been discussed at some length by others.[32]

In case it is thought that I am unfairly singling out Christianity's failure when, in fact, the environmental dangers we face are the result of the thoughtlessness and greed of humanity in every part of the world, I would like to point out that, while there may be some merit in recognizing that environmental degradation is universal, it is still the case that the West's impact on the environment is considerably greater than that of the rest of the world put together. This was acknowledged recently in a public address by the Vice-President of the United States, Mr Al Gore, well-known as a committed environmentalist himself. Addressing a meeting of the 53 nations that constitute the Unites Nations Commission on Sustainable Development, he said that 'a child born in the United States will have, in his or her lifetime, 30 times more impact on the earth's environment than a child born in India'.[33] While that does not excuse the Indian child from using nature and its resources more responsibly, it certainly places a much greater burden on his/her American, and Western, counterpart. And the burden ultimately falls on the political, economic and religious institutions responsible for the upbringing of these children.

And that is where Christianity's failure becomes glaring. For I cannot help wondering what difference it might have made to the state of the world today, had Christianity been able to retain and promote the ascetic side of the teachings of Jesus, St Paul, Augustine and a host of other Christian luminaries. It certainly seems that Christianity became involved in power and the pursuit of political patronage far too early in its infancy, thus coming under some pressure to shed its other-worldly emphases. It cannot be just incidental that even Augustine's great work, *The City of God*, was undertaken primarily to show that the fall of the Roman empire could not have been the fault of Christianity! This defensiveness, developed so early, perhaps made it easier for much of Christianity – apart, that is, from its monastic cults – to 'cohabit' with the secular pursuit of power, wealth and pleasure. And this cohabitation over the centuries obscured the ascetic side of its origins so completely that by the time in its theological development that Albert Schweitzer appeared on the scene, it has been ever so proud to emphasize its 'world-and-life-affirming' character by contrast with Eastern religions.[34] And this happened despite Weber's pronouncement, a good deal earlier, that Hindu society's failure to develop the kind of industrial capitalism that prevailed in modern Europe, was because the Hindu religion did not lend itself to 'rational worldly asceticism'. As Trevor Ling paraphrases Weber's argument: '. . . Hindu religion lacked the kind of ethic which would lead to "rational worldly asceticism", and therefore had failed to effect that transition to industrial capitalism, in which, according to Weber, the Protestant ethic had in Europe played a significant part.'[35] Which of these two eminent gentlemen was right about Indian religion, and society? Perhaps neither. Perhaps it does not matter, here anyway.

What does matter is this. The will-to-live and to seek one's own happiness is too powerful a force, in and by itself, to need affirmation by religion, or anything else. Teaching denial and sacrifice, 'desirelessness' and 'dying to this world' – that, however, needs to be done, deliberately and incessantly; and the only institution that can do that is religion. The rational worldly asceticism that Weber speaks of is, in my opinion, as much a corollary as a condition of the kingdom of God. Capitalism, with its attendant consumerism, undermines it, and, in so doing, threatens at least the 'quality of life', if not the very continuity of human life and society as we know it. It is always risky to answer questions about what might have been, but, in fact, was not. But the risks notwithstanding, I cannot help raising some questions. What if religion, instead of being an ally of capitalism and the political establishment, had been its foe, vigorously preaching its message of dying to this world and desirelessness? What if it had succeeded in instilling in us greater respect for nature by preaching that we were only guests or borrowers in the world, 'stewards' perhaps, but never masters? If its message of selflessness had succeeded in significantly curbing our greed and selfishness, would there have been more of the 'economic pie' produced by capitalism left to be distributed? And if religion's message of compassion and caring for the needy had made a greater impact on humanity, would more of this pie have gone to where the need was greatest, thus reducing disparities and helping build a just society?

10 The Ethic of Rights and the Ethic of Duties

My discussion so far of social justice (especially in Chapter 4) should have shown us that, at its heart, it is liberal in conception. Liberals of various persuasions may disagree about some of the details, but what they all agree on is the primacy of justice among virtues; that is to say that, among other things, justice, fairness and individual rights play a commanding role in the organization and functioning of a liberal society. Equally importantly, in a liberal social order there are no *a priori* ends, but only those that individuals constituting it freely choose to pursue. The tacit social contract that it presupposes is that any individual is free to pursue his/her own personal interests, as long as, and to the extent that, it does not unduly obstruct the personal interests pursued by all the others in this society. It, therefore, does not legislate what interests individuals might pursue but only how the interests of all are to be regulated. It is for this reason that liberal theories tend to concentrate on procedural justice – namely, rules and principles whose adoption would be most likely to enable each member of society to get the maximum possible satisfaction of his/her interests, consistent with a similar outcome for all. There is a clear sense in which such liberalism provides the ideal framework for capitalist free enterprise, that is, the pursuit of private profit and wealth. And this has not been the least of the merits sustaining it in its dominant social role in Western democracies, since its emergence in the doctrines and ideas of Hobbes, Locke and others. But it would be wrong to think that its main intellectual or moral appeal rests in its ability to buttress capitalism. Far from it, in fact.

What sustains the lure of liberalism is its truly emancipating vision of the human person – the uncompromising priority it places on the autonomy, that is, the freedom and dignity of every individual human being. This freedom belongs to individuals solely in virtue of their being rational and will remain theirs, and only theirs, as long as they do not foolishly squander their rationality. This idea of individual autonomy is a quintessentially Enlightenment idea, and, in the words of perhaps its greatest exponent, Kant, can be summed up as follows:

> Enlightenment is man's release from his self-incurred tutelage. Tutelage is man's inability to make use of his understanding without direction from another. Self-incurred is their tutelage when its cause lies not in

lack of reason but in lack of resolution and courage to use it without direction from another. *Sapere aude!* 'Have courage to use your own reason!' – that is the motto of enlightenment. Laziness and cowardice are the reasons why so great a portion of mankind, after nature has long since discharged them from external direction (*naturaliter maiorennes*), nevertheless remain under lifelong tutelage, and why it is so easy for others to set themselves up as their guardians. It is so easy not to be of age. If I have a book which understands for me, a pastor who has a conscience for me, a physician who decides my diet, and so forth, I need not trouble myself. I need not think, if I can only pay – others will readily undertake the irksome work for me.[1]

When one reflects how in history, in every age and everywhere, self-appointed 'guardians' of umpteen kinds have presumed to tell the many what to do, and how awful the price of refusal has generally been – then, and only then, does one come to appreciate fully the liberating vision of liberalism. And it's not that these 'guardians' have, by any means, ceased to be born in recent days: apart from the traditional ones – the Brahmin and the mullah, the pope and the padre – there are a whole host of newly emerging 'experts' and 'professionals' who would love to have us do their bidding from the cradle to the grave. The Enlightenment, and its offspring, liberalism, for the first time in human history, made it theoretically possible for each individual, irrespective of birth, wealth, colour of skin, religion and gender – to throw away this yoke of tutelage by simply beginning to exercise their freedom.

Had liberalism been just a great vision, incapable of being put into practice, it would still have commanded worthy mention as a noble utopia. But the fact is that it has been the dominant political force in the West for well over two centuries. It not only provided the inspiration for the French revolution, it also influenced powerfully, first, American independence, and, then, the American constitution, through its immense impact on the thinking of the founding fathers of America. It was largely responsible for the abolition of slavery and, later, for the movement for desegregation and the granting of civil rights for blacks in America, and for oppressed minorities around the world; it lies at the heart of the United Nations Declaration of Human Rights, now inspiring the powerful women's rights movements across the world and giving rise to other struggles, such as for gay rights, children's rights and a host of others, including some that the originators of liberalism might not have thought of, for example, animal rights. In other words, without the emancipating vision of liberalism that every human being has dignity and, therefore, certain inalienable rights, many of the profound social revolutions in modern history might not have been possible at all. It is true that the socialist power block, led by the former Soviet Union, had an immense influence on the decolonization of much of the 'third world'. But the socialism of Marx and Engels itself presupposes, and builds on, some of the liberating sentiments of liberalism.

It is, in my opinion, very hard to exaggerate the importance of liberalism, whether as an idea or as a tool of actual social transformation in history. But, after the richly deserved eulogy has been delivered, it has to be said that all is not well with the liberal view of things. This may have been evident for a long time, but has been brought into sharper focus by the intense debate that has gone on in the academic world for the last twenty odd years around John Rawls' *A Theory of Justice*. This work, while, arguably, providing by far the most powerful defence of liberalism since Kant, has, at the same time, exposed some of its obvious weaknesses. It should be worth our while, in our own larger context, to highlight some of these. The form of liberalism that Rawls advocates, along with Kant, is best described as 'deontological'. Deontological liberalism is distinguished from other forms of liberalism in ascribing overriding primacy to justice among all moral and political ideals. This primacy, at one level, entails that the demands of justice and individual rights always take precedence over other moral and political considerations. But, as Michael Sandel points out, the primacy of justice in this 'moral sense alone' is not what distinguishes deontological liberalism from other varieties, such as those of John Stuart Mill or John Locke, who also emphasize the importance of justice and individual rights:

> On the full deontological view, the primacy of justice describes not only a moral priority but also a privileged form of justification; the right is prior to the good not only in that its claims take precedence, but also in that its principles are independently derived. This means that, unlike other practical injunctions, principles of justice are justified in a way that does not depend on any particular vision of the good. To the contrary: given its independent status, the right constrains the good and sets its bounds. 'The concept of good and evil is not defined prior to the moral law, to which, it would seem, the former would have to serve as foundation; rather the concept of good and evil must be defined after and by means of the law' (Kant 1788:65).[2]

In the words of John Rawls himself: 'The parties to the original position do not agree on what the moral facts are, as if there were already such facts. It is not that, being situated impartially, they have a clear and undistorted view of a prior and independent moral order. Rather (for constructivism), there is no such order, and, therefore, no such facts apart from the procedure as a whole.'[3] This deontology implies that there is no moral order suffusing the universe: the order is invented, or rather constructed, by its inhabitants as they go along. There are no pre-existing ends: persons create their own ends, and society is a community of independent individuals, each primarily pursuing his or her own ends; and only secondarily that of others, because of the requirements of the 'social compact' that exists among rational individuals. It is not surprising that the 'kingdom of ends' that such individuals collectively create is frequently the sum of the lowest common denominators among our objects of interest, for example, pleasure, wealth, power, fame and so on, rather than the cultivation of any noble virtues or of what Kant calls the 'good will'. As Sandel remarks:

> What goes on behind the veil of ignorance is not a contract or an agreement but if anything a kind of discovery; and what goes on in 'purely preferential choice' is less a choosing of ends than a matching of pre-existing desires, undifferentiated as to worth, with the best available means of satisfying them. For the parties to the original position, as for the parties to ordinary deliberative rationality, the liberating moment fades before it arrives: the sovereign subject is left at sea in the circumstances it was thought to command.[4]

It may indeed be the case that the liberating project of deontology could not even get launched unless the individuals entering this social contract brought with them heavy baggages of morals and values derived from other institutions such as religion. Perhaps that is why the weakening of religion and of the moral constraints that it teaches, turns the social fabric of liberal democracies into mindless hedonism, consumerism and a 'war of each on all'.

An equally troublesome implication of deontological liberalism seems to be the view of the self that it presupposes. The identity of the self in this scheme is determined quite independently of the interests and attachments we have, the history and community of which they are parts and the relationships they enjoy with their friends, family, church, or sect, and so on. For they have the 'moral power to form, to revise, and rationally to pursue a conception of the good': their autonomy derives just from being rational. And, in any case, the veil of ignorance requires that the parties to the original position do not know in advance either their own interests, attachments and place in society or those of the others entering into the contract. 'But', in the words of Sandel, again:

We cannot regard ourselves as independent in this way without great cost to those loyalties and convictions whose moral force consists partly in the fact that living by them is inseparable from understanding ourselves as the particular persons we are – as members of this family or community or nation or people, as bearers of this history, as sons and daughters of that revolution, as citizens of this republic. Allegiances such as these are more than values I happen to have or aims I 'espouse at any given time'. They go beyond the obligations I voluntarily incur and the 'natural duties' I owe to human beings as such. They allow that to some I owe more than justice requires or even permits, not by reason of agreements I have made but instead in virtue of those more or less enduring attachments and commitments which taken together partly define the person I am.[5]

This view of the self may not only be faulty in theory, but also dangerous in practice. For the deliberate alienation from so much of oneself that the veil requires, not unnaturally, promotes the alienation from the very society and its institutions that the contract may have been designed to safeguard and buttress.

A particular implication of this view of the self and the universe, discussed above, may be what James Fishkin calls the 'trilemma' of justice, equal opportunity and the family.[6] Very briefly, this trilemma – that is, 'a dilemma with three corners' – arises because the liberal conception of justice, which recognizes the two principles of merit and equal opportunity, can only allow for the autonomy of the family if it is willing to sacrifice at least one of those principles. That is to say that not all three can be accommodated together. In Fishkin's words:

Once the role of the family is taken into account, the apparently moderate aspiration of equal opportunity produces conflicts with the private sphere of liberty – with autonomous family relations – that are nothing short of intractable. Elements that are essential to the liberal doctrine of equal opportunity come into irreconcilable conflict with the private core of the notion of liberty, the portion that touches most of our lives most directly.[7]

Fishkin defines these principles as follows:

1. 'The Principle Of Merit': 'There should be widespread procedural fairness in the evaluation of qualifications for positions.'[8]
2. 'Equality of Life Chances' (as a more adequate rendering of 'equal opportunity'): 'The prospects of children for eventual positions in society should not vary in any systematic and significant manner with their arbitrary native characteristics.'[9]

3. 'Autonomy of the Family': 'Consensual relations within a given family governing the development of its children should not be coercibly interfered with except to insure for the children the essential prerequisites for adult participation in society.'[10]

The conflict between any two of these principles with the third can be seen arising through the following paraphrase. According to the first of these, a just society is one where people occupy positions strictly in virtue of their qualifications for doing the job properly, and not by virtue of non-relevant characteristics such as skin colour, race, gender, or sexual orientation. The second principle is designed to ensure the structural fairness of the society, so that by merely looking at, say, a number of babies in a hospital ward, we should not be able to predict what sort of positions in society these children might occupy as adults, as is actually the case still in most existing societies. We know that in Western societies black-skinned children will find it very much more difficult to reach high-wage, high-prestige positions; or that in India children born in low-caste families will be, generally, unable even today to occupy socially prominent positions. The third principle, however, in recognition of the family's liberty to maximize the life chances of children born inside it, must allow it to use its existing advantages, say, wealth and power, to enhance the qualifications of the children for high positions by sending them, for example, to expensive preparatory schools – thereby ensuring the possession of greater skills on the part of these children for high positions. The family's autonomy allows the use of existing advantages to tilt the merit pool in its own favour, which, of course, can only obstruct the principle of equality of life chances for all. It seems to me that liberalism's failure, or reluctance, to appreciate the force of this trilemma may be due to its rather 'sanitized' view of the self which does not recognize family, friendships or other attachments as part of the full identity of the self.

This diminished understanding of the self that underpins liberalism has some rather disastrous consequences in practical politics. Devoid of any moral or spiritual purpose, or even a rich enough conception of the universe or of history, the liberal self can only pursue practical politics as being almost entirely concerned with social justice, rather narrowly construed. Its narrowness has two concrete manifestations. Firstly, the excessive individualism of liberal politics distorts the true character of politics itself by failing to recognize that politics is, almost by definition, a community-based enterprise, that it has to do, essentially, with the 'polis'. Communitarian thinkers have quite justifiably accused liberalism of this failure, while emphasizing the value in politics of participation, deliberation, civic virtues and of education as their foundation. With varying emphases, Sandel, Taylor, Putnam and Etzioni have all made this, or a somewhat similar criticism of liberal individualism.[11] Secondly, the rights-based approach to social life that liberalism encourages – not only because of the individualism, but also because of the primacy of justice and rights that it espouses – tends, on the whole, towards the development of endemically conflict-ridden societies. Wherever the language of rights predominates, conflict tends always to be brewing, and violence is always potentially round the corner, if not out on the streets already.

In a sense, whatever the nature of the political order or ideology, individualism, greed, conflict and violence are bound, as a matter of fact, to manifest themselves in social transactions from time to time. This is because it does seem, contingently, to be the case that humans have a tendency to display these vices. What is different in the context of liberalism is that these vices cannot plausibly be viewed merely as contingent, sporadic outbursts of irrationality or selfishness. Liberalism may seem to give them 'official' sanction not only through its failure to offer a sublime ideal capable of restraining these tendencies but by making the individual and individual rights the principal determinants of political activity. Communitarian thinking on the relationship between individuals and society has always been quite explicit on the dangers of pure individualism. According to David Schuman,

> As one strand of thinkers from Aristotle to Rousseau to Marx has noted, a people obsessed with individual rights will suffer a predictable pathology. Because a right comes into play only when an individual asserts it and thus assumes a pugnacious stance towards fellow-citizens, a politics grounded in rights will be a politics of separation, exclusion and alienation. The prime objective will not be to find common ground – but to impose your will on others. As the 19th century French thinker Alexis de Tocqueville noted, this attitude 'saps the virtues of public life, reducing it to little more than an adversarial market transaction'.[12]

It ought to be acknowledged at this point, simply as a matter of accuracy, though not only for that reason, that Kant, the best known exponent of liberalism, at least in theory, avoids the pitfalls noted above which the current practice of liberalism embraces, perhaps unwittingly. This has to be said because Kant is not only emphatic on the importance of the community and of education in politics. He is equally insistent on making it clear that, since all rights ultimately spring from the categorical imperative, rights must always be understood and spoken of against the backdrop of duties, of morality. Here, for example, is an unambiguous statement regarding the relationship between rights and duties:

> Inasmuch as duties and rights are related to each other, why is moral (*Moral*) philosophy usually (for example, by Cicero) labeled the theory of duties and not also of rights? The reason for this is that we know our own freedom (from which all moral laws and hence all rights as well as duties are derived) only through the moral imperative, which is a proposition commanding duties; the capacity to obligate others to a duty, that is the concept of a right, can be subsequently derived from this imperative.[13]

Similarly, on the importance of the community, Kant leaves us in no doubt whatsoever. Talking about the three forms of the state – autocratic, aristocratic and democratic – for example, he says that 'The three authorities in the state that proceed out of the concept of a commonwealth in general (*res publica lattices dicta*) are nothing more than so many relationships in the united Will of the people, which originates *a priori* in reason.'[14] And, later, he adds: 'Every free republic is and can be nothing else than a representative system of the people if it is to protect the rights of its citizens in the name of the people. Under a representative system, these rights are protected by the citizens themselves, united and acting through their representatives (deputies).'[15] But Kant is more than merely aware that for republican forms of government to emerge, people need to be made ready. Hence the importance of education, especially of what Kant calls 'cosmopolitan education'.[16] In his *Religion within the Limits of Reason Alone*, Kant exhorts us to abandon what he calls the 'ethical state of nature' in order to become members of an 'ethical commonwealth'. And the reason why this is necessary is as follows:

> Just as the juridical state of nature is one of war of every man against every other, so too is the ethical state of nature one in which the good principle, which resides in each man, is continually attacked by the evil which is found in him and also in everyone else. Men . . . mentally corrupt one another's moral dispositions; despite the good will of each individual, yet, because they lack a principle which unites them, they recede through their dissensions, from the common goal of goodness and, just as though they were *instruments of evil*, expose one another to the risk of falling once again under the sovereignty of the evil principle.[17]

That is why rational beings must leave this ethical state of nature and together establish the ethical commonwealth:

Now here we have a duty which is *sui generis*, not of men towards men, but of the human race towards itself. For the species of rational beings is objectively, in the idea of reason, destined for a social goal, namely, the promotion of the highest as a social good. But because the highest moral good cannot be achieved merely by the exertions of the single individual towards his own moral perfection, but requires rather a union of such individuals into a whole towards the same goal – into a system of well-disposed men, in which and through whose unity alone the highest moral good can come to pass – the idea of such a whole as a universal republic based on laws of virtue, is an idea completely distinguished from all moral laws (which concern what we know to lie in our own power); since it involves working towards a whole regarding which we do not know whether, as such, it lies in our power or not.[18]

It would seem, then, that the problems of liberalism, that we discussed in the earlier part of this chapter, may only be the problems of current liberal practice, not of the liberal vision, when taken as a whole and presented at its best, as exemplified in Kant, for instance. Important though this might be if it were a fact, I now wish to move to something more relevant to my larger aim in this book. And that is this. It seems to me that what I called the metaphysical-religious theories of justice, in Chapter 1, and which seem to be embedded especially in the idea of the kingdom of God (including its counterparts in non-theistic religions) are the opposite of liberal justice, especially that of deontological liberalism, as reviewed above, on practically all important counts. As we have seen, the former do postulate entities, properties or processes whose existence is required for the derivation of the concept and principles of justice. There are pre-existing ends and an act or principle is just only insofar as it promotes those ends, for example, helps prepare for the kingdom of God or the reign of *dharma*, and so on. Even non-theistic religions, such as Theravada Buddhism and certain schools of Hinduism, see the world as governed by *dharma*, the counterpart of *logos*, at the level of nature, and by *karma*, the 'law of moral causation' at the human and animal levels. Given this, humans do not create their own ends as they go along: they try, or fail, to achieve pre-established ends – *mokṣa* or *nirvāṇa* in the Indian religions and salvation or submission to God's will in the biblical religions. The social order in the world is not, and cannot be, the consequence of a social contract among individuals – either actual or hypothetical; and the only 'veil of ignorance' that can be spoken of in the context of religions does not describe the conditions under which the social contract would be made, but those ontological forces that entrap humans into their bondage to false views of reality and false values on earth. These false views and the false values do, as a matter of fact, result in excessive egoism, self-love and pride on the part of humans. But, unlike liberalism, which makes autonomy and individualism their creed, religions regard these as delusions and sin. Our souls, indeed, are autonomous – except in Advaita Vedanta – because they are immortal and unique to each individual. But the perfected state of the souls lies not in self-love or economic or political freedom, but either in loving submission to God, or in a desireless isolation and serenity, or, as in Advaita Vedanta, in the merger of the *ātman*, the individual soul, into the *Brahman* the 'universal' soul.

Nor is the embodied soul merely any kind of transcendental subject, without character, emotions, interests, loyalties and attachments – the condition of the individual in the 'veil of ignorance' postulated by deontological liberalism. Quite its opposite, in fact. Humans, as it happens, have an excess of these 'afflictions' already; that is the very core of sinfulness and *samsāra*, conditions to be overcome for the attainment of salvation. And when salvation is reached, one is no longer a political creature in need of a social contract. The only 'contract' that religion envisages is a set of obligations to society, to the church, the *sangha* and the *dharma* determined by one's place in the social order, caste, clan, *varna* or class. And the latter are not artificial constructs brought into being by some contrived collective human arrangement, but very much part of the divine, or other ontologically determined, order outside which humans can have no being at all. The 'community', then, not only shapes, but defines the individual; and, for that very reason, 'constitutes' it – not just in the weaker, sociological sense of 'nurturing', but in the stronger sense of providing the *raison d'être* for an individual's being – who he or she is and what his or her role and functions are.

The only 'equal opportunity' in this scheme of things lies in the fact that, in principle, we are all equally entitled to salvation, or that we are all 'equal in the eyes of God'. So, while equality in principle does exist at the spiritual level, even at that level, there is no 'equality of outcome', since not all of us might, in fact, break through the obstacles of sin and *samsāra*. At the material level, there is no equality of any kind, for the very good reason that the existing inequalities cannot be regarded as accidental. They may, in fact, have been designed by the powers-that-be as constitutive of the 'testing-ground' that the earthly order must be. Neither wealth nor poverty, neither earthly power nor political deprivation are barriers to spiritual salvation. Nor can they be conditions for it. This does not imply that out of love or compassion or filial, or other, duty, we may not try to alleviate the physical suffering caused by material deprivation, or the spiritual blindness caused by excessive wealth. But religion should not encourage the view that material equality can be its preoccupation: religion just is not about equality of opportunity or outcome in the material realm. And the 'principle of merit' is a postulate of common-sense rather than a requirement of religious piety.

It also seems to me that religion very clearly enshrines an ethic of duties rather than an ethic of rights. At the very least, it is much closer to the Kantian view of the relationship between rights and duties than to the popular practice of liberal politics. In a world governed by God's power, there can be no absolute rights for anyone without compromising the ultimate authority of God. To the extent there are any rights, however, they must, as in Kant's system, be derivable only from our duties – to God and to his creatures. And duties, therefore – not rights – must be the operative principle in a divinely ordered universe, as also in one governed by *dharma* or *logos*. Every individual must diligently perform his or her *dharma*; and if that is done, rights will be taken care of automatically. For injustice *is* the decline of *dharma* in the natural order and the dereliction of duty in the moral order, by the individuals and classes constituting society: *dharma* as law and *dharma* as duty are prior to, and the preconditions of, any relative rights we may have in this world.

Finally, I wish to conclude this chapter with a remark on Kant, again. It is true that Kant draws a lot from the history, language and symbolism of Christianity: he was, after all, a very good Lutheran. But I still think that his liberalism can only mistakenly be regarded as Christian in its origins. Although his 'ethical commonwealth' no doubt is partially derived from the idea of the kingdom of God, he says quite clearly in a long note after using the latter term, 'Here a kingdom of God is represented not according to a particular covenant (i.e. not Messianic) but *moral* (knowable through unassisted reason).'[19] Moreover, it is important to remember that according to him, Christianity, as other historical or revealed religions, is an example of 'Ecclesiastical Faith', whereas the religion he clearly favours, 'pure religious faith', is a product of reason. Finally, the autonomy of the individual that he so stoutly defends seems, in his own view, to be incompatible with a theistic religious framework, because this autonomy entails that a rational being can be 'obedient only to those laws which he himself gives'.[20] Kant may have been a Christian, but he was, above all, a leader of the 'age of Enlightenment'!

11 Conclusion: The City of God and the Citadel of Creatures

One of the burdens of my arguments in the preceding pages has been to show – in ways direct and indirect – why social justice cannot be said to be the main concern of religion. That does not mean that it cannot raise its voice against, say, apartheid in South Africa, the violation of human rights in China or 'ethnic cleansing', supposedly being perpetrated in Bosnia-Herzegovina. I do not suggest that religion should, or could, be utterly indifferent to questions of justice: that it be 'colour-blind' to injustice in the world. For religion does have a prophetic and a pastoral role. Also, even accepting the principle of the separation of religion, on the one hand, and state and politics, on the other, we have seen that actually keeping them apart, in practice, is not easy; although, in my opinion, that must remain the aim of all concerned. What I wish to maintain, primarily, is that religion must not become, or be seen as, the instrument of social justice, in its more technical sense of distributive, economic and political justice; whether such a programme is proposed or carried out under Marxist or liberal inspiration. The most important reason for my view is that construing religion in this way takes religion away from its main goals – the moral and spiritual transformation of humanity – and, at the same time, leads to its adoption of the ideology of liberalism, which, as a utopia, is quite the opposite of that enshrined in the idea of the kingdom of God.

The economic and political equality of individuals (as against their moral and spiritual equality) is a liberal idea arising out of the Enlightenment vision of humans and their place in the universe. This vision incorporates individualism, secularism, rationalism and the pursuit of 'happiness', hedonistically understood – with the *rights* of individuals counting as inviolable, inalienable, and so on. And, as I tried to show in the last chapter, particularly, this utopia is, in most essential respects, the opposite of that cherished by religion. An important point of caution must be recorded here. If the reasonably detailed critique of deontological liberalism, as particularly represented by Rawls, which was offered in the last chapter, were to lead someone to think that liberalism was not much of an adversary of the religious vision of things, that would be a mistake. For liberalism, as a whole, commands a much wider, and richer, array of ideas and emphases. Rawls may be the most influential of liberals today, perhaps; but there are many other illustrious liberals that any opponent of liberalism has to contend with. Even within the narrow confines of deontological liberalism, Kant may, in my opinion, be less susceptible to some of the criticisms of liberalism, as I tried to indicate in the last chapter.

More importantly, there is another, a more extended, sense of the term 'liberal' – the sense, namely, in which it is 'syncretistic' among the various versions of liberalism, such as those of Hobbes and Locke; Mill and Hume; and Kant and Rawls, and so on. Although there are well-known, and important differences among these formulations, they are still all liberal. The sense of 'liberal' I have in mind here is well expressed by Jeremy Waldron, in his 'Theoretical Foundations of Liberalism', as follows:

> The terms 'socialism', 'conservatism', and 'liberalism' are like surnames and the theories, principles and parties that share one of these names often do not have much more in common with one another than the members of a widely extended family. If we examine the range of views that are classified under any one of these labels, we may find what Wittgenstein referred to in another context as 'a complicated network of similarities overlapping and criss-crossing . . . sometimes overall similarities, sometimes similarities of detail'; but we are unlikely to find any set of doctrines or principles that are held in common by all of them, any single cluster of theoretical and practical propositions that might be regarded as the *core* or the *essence* of the ideology in question.
> . . . Liberal moderatism fades into conservatism; the conservative's concern for community matches the socialist's; the socialist claims to take the liberal concern for freedom more seriously than the liberals themselves; and so on.[1]

Liberalism, understood in this way, is, I maintain, a unique vision of individuals and of a just social order, which cannot be subsumed under any other utopian vision – certainly not that encapsulated in the idea of the kingdom of God. In fact, as I have indicated earlier, more than once, the two visions are antithetical. I can imagine it being suggested here that, although liberalism may be unique, that, by itself, does not explain why we ought to take its vision seriously. My answer to this would be to refer the reader back to my 'eulogy' on liberalism delivered in the last chapter. To recapitulate it briefly, liberalism has to be taken seriously because it encapsulates a powerfully lofty vision of individual rights and dignity, which, once it has taken root, can, at worst, perhaps be suppressed momentarily, but never eradicated altogether: because humanity at large, once it has experienced liberalism's liberating ethos, will never let go of it, for long. Am I overstating the power of liberalism here? Perhaps; but I myself do not think so. In any case, even if I am wrong in my assessment of the appeal of the liberal vision in the long run, there seems, in my mind, no doubt about its hold on thinking minds today – not just in the West, but also, perhaps, in the rest of the world.

I am of the opinion that Leroy S. Rouner's recently raised question, 'Is There a Global Ethic?'[2] can be answered affirmatively by pointing out that, at least for the moment, liberalism is the nearest to a global ethic we can claim to have. My reasons for maintaining this position are not just that the major democracies in the world are based on liberal foundations and that the principles and practices of the United Nations Organization, especially its Declaration of Human Rights, are largely based on those same foundations; although these are important pointers in that direction. As additional evidence, one may point to the success of the 'universalists' in fighting off those countries which wished to define human rights in religious, cultural, economic and social terms, at the recent World Conference on Human Rights held in Vienna.[3] It may be wrong to overstate the importance of the 'victory' – won, as it was, as much by the economic and political might of the West as by any other means. But it would be equally wrong not to record it as a significant event, since the victory was achieved despite a sustained opposition from a powerful array of nations, such as China, Cuba, Syria, Iran, Vietnam, Pakistan, Malaysia, Singapore, Yemen and Indonesia, among many others.[4] In this context, it ought to be recorded as an important event that at the recent meeting of the Parliament of the World's Religions, held in Chicago, a concerted effort was made – under the leadership of Dr Hans Kung and others, and blessed by such eminent religious figures as the Dalai Lama – to draw up a 'Global Ethic'.[5] Although its final details are, to the best of my knowledge, still being worked out, it seems to me that until such a document is endorsed by all of the world's major religious faiths, liberalism would continue to provide the nearest approximation to a global ethic. And even in the event of that endorsement taking place, I doubt that it would carry much conviction if it failed to incorporate the main elements of the UN Declaration on Human Rights, for example, which, as I mentioned earlier, is closely based on the liberal vision of humans and their place in the world.

Be that as it may, this vision – at least its contemporary practice – is, as I tried to show in the last chapter, somewhat narrow and incomplete in itself. Destitute of pre-existing, higher moral and spiritual ends, its individualist core, with its emphasis on rights, rather than obligations, helps create a 'fortress mentality', so that in a purely liberal setting, individuals, and even groups, could potentially, if not actually, be in a state of war, of each against all. The sovereignty of reason that it postulates – while admirable in some ways (for example, in excluding paternalism) – in other important ways, overestimates the power of reason by failing, for example, to acknowledge how reasoning can easily turn into rationalization, or, at best, into a purely prudential cost-benefit analysis. Reason may be a good slave, but perhaps a bad sovereign.

In theory, at least, Kant may be said to be better equipped to deal with these criticisms of liberalism, as I tried to show in the last chapter. Being a good Lutheran, he is certainly well aware of the corruptibility and pettiness of humans. And, equally certainly, he does not think that, without an awful lot of political or 'cosmopolitan' education, people will be able to maintain a republic, not to mention an ethical community of ends. But, nonetheless, in his very high expectations of education itself, he perhaps betrays an innocence of how, without high moral and spiritual convictions, such as his own, reason can become a tool of petty concerns – greed, selfishness and the pursuit of profit and power, frequently without much regard to the interests of the community at large. It seems to me that liberalism, even at its best, is 'utopian' in a not-so-desirable sense of the term, implying as it does, a great, but flawed vision, incapable of being fully realized; because it rests on unrealistic and inadequate foundations.

Many of these features of the more adequate Kantian formulation of liberalism have been recently brought into sharper focus by communitarian thinkers, referred to in the last chapter. They, quite correctly, try to soften the harsh individualism of the liberal view of things by emphasizing the origin of rights in and through the community and of the importance of moral and social responsibility, political education, and citizenship. Some elements of this kind of thinking were in evidence, for example, in Sandel's critique of liberalism reviewed in the last chapter. This communitarian emphasis is welcome, indeed, and good as far as it goes. But my suspicion is that it does not – perhaps cannot – go far enough. For communitarianism, without a religious grounding, remains an emphasis within liberalism, in the end, to be revived from time to time, but never quite succeeding in imparting to the community that aura of 'sacredness' that religion manages to, so easily. If the origins of the community do not have divine, or other transcendent, sanction; and if its morality is not absolute for similar reasons; then the feeling of communal responsibility, and so on, is always vulnerable to collapse under the driving force of the very individualism that liberalism promotes: that would seem to be the lesson to be learnt from the practice of liberalism today. For religion, however, the community is not something that just provides a much needed counterweight to individualism. The congregation and the church, *varṇa* (and caste), *dharma* and *sangha* represent the sacred order of being; and the eternal and sacred laws that govern them can only be flouted by an individual at his own peril. It is no accident, then, that most of the continuing and healthy communities surviving in the world today are still those that originally formed around religions. Nor is it surprising, for example, that Robert Owen, the famous utopian socialist and communitarian, looked at American religious communities as models for the socialist communities he wished to build. There may, then, be more than a plausible case for the view that religion may be a better tool for building the kind of community that the communitarian emphasis within liberalism espouses. Having said that, however, one must also candidly acknowledge the shortcomings of traditional religious communities, particularly their conformism and rigidity. The obverse side of a community based on sacred and eternal laws may well be its inability to countenance innovation and the freedom to rebel against mindless and, sometimes, cruel goals pursued by the community. And neither religion, nor any other form of communitarianism that I know of, is able to provide any shield against the tyranny of the community itself against individuals, witnessed so regularly in history. Only liberalism does that.

But what, then, can serve as the much-needed counterweight to the excesses or privations of liberalism? There may surely be many answers of a philosophical kind. But, in my opinion, religion, or more specifically, the religious utopia of the kingdom of God (and its equivalents), can do that, at least as well as any other alternative I can think of that might be considered practicable today. The idea of the kingdom not only provides the moral high ground, more specifically the altruism (and I do not mean 'as-if-altruism', but the 'real thing'!), which can keep capitalism humane. It might also alleviate the excessive individualism of liberalism by emphasizing the sinfulness (*avidyā*) inherent in self-love. It preaches the ethic of duty, of love and compassion, as against that of rights, and thus helps contain our belligerence and intolerance. It weans us away from obsession with happiness, hedonistically construed, in this world, by emphasizing that 'happiness' (beatitudo, blessedness, *mokṣa*, *nirvāṇa*) cannot be achieved in this life;[6] and thus might help to give the world a chance to survive annihilation through unrestrained consumption and thoughtless exploitation of nature. It instils in us the spirit of love, compassion, *bhūta-hitatva* (the well-being of all creatures) – the spirit that while not directly pursuing social justice as such, still has the effect of producing a fairer state of affairs on earth; and which, at the same time, firmly turns our heads toward higher, transcendental goals.

But this utopia also, if left to itself, can become sterile, unimaginative, unadventurous, destructive of genuine individual freedom and creativity and unable to resist the tyranny of the power-seeking Brahmin, mullah, priest or padre, or of a deranged religious fanatic imposing his will on people in the guise of God's commands. History is full of instances of all these. My conclusion, then, is that, for the maximum good of humanity at large, both utopias are needed: two visions, two kingdoms, two 'cities', two realms. Between them, they provide for rights and duties; individuals and (divinely ordained) communities; self-love and salvation; the terrestrial and the celestial; self-assertion and sacrifice; liberal social justice and the kingdom of God; the fortress or 'citadel' of creatures and the city of God.

But I do not at all mean to suggest any kind of 'wedding' or even friendship between these two utopias. The only logical relationship between them can be one of tension, opposition, antagonism, hostility. What Augustine says of the differences between the city of God and the earthly city, quoted in Chapter 9, may be said to sum up the opposition in principle between the utopias: the love of God characterizing the kingdom of God, and self-love being the driving force of the liberal vision. One cannot be a substitute for the other any more than it can be an instrument of the other. I cannot help quoting Luther here, who, talking about the spiritual kingdom of Christ, on the one hand, and the secular kingdom of the world, on the other, had this to say on the interdependence of the two realms: '(T)hese two kingdoms must be sharply distinguished, and both be permitted to remain; the one to produce piety, the other to bring about external peace and prevent evil deeds; neither is sufficient in the world without the other.'[7] I would like to end by suggesting that, like the two kingdoms spoken of above by Luther, both utopias – that of the kingdom of God and the liberal vision of a just society – be permitted to remain; the one to produce piety and the other to bring about social justice on earth. Neither may be sufficient in the world without the other.

Lest my conclusion regarding the coexistence of the two conflicting utopias, however, be seen as a mere pious platitude, I must hasten to add precisely what I mean. Who am I directing my recommendation to? Surely not to the deeply committed on either side of the divide, for they would not, as a matter of rule, wish even to countenance the other? Perhaps then, my hope is that the uncommitted, or the mildly committed, may be able to appreciate the value of the insights and contributions of each towards the well-being of humanity at large. Yes, but I think that my optimism may be of a more 'insidious' kind, if I may put it that way. For I start from the premise that even the most committed, on either side, may have some moments of doubt or hesitation about the adequacy, or even the truth, of their positions. In the case of the liberals, it is, I should have thought, to be expected: a liberal with a completely closed mind would seem to me to be a strange creature, indeed! And we all know that some of the most devoutly religious personages in history have had their moments of doubt, Jesus Christ among them; his anguished question about why his father seemed to have forsaken him, may be evidence of that doubt! My hope, then, is that the committed, while as a general rule hostile to the other vision, would, at least in those exceptional moments of doubt, permit themselves to contemplate that it may have something of value to offer.

But perhaps this scepticism, even rare moments of it, is not required for my conclusion to be appreciated. What may, in fact, be sufficient is a certain kind of 'wisdom' on the part of the committed. The kind of wisdom I have in mind was, I think, displayed in abundant measure by the founding fathers of America, who, despite the fact that they were all religious, in various ways and to varying degrees, went on, nonetheless, to lay the foundations of a liberal society. As another example, one may mention Mahatma Gandhi who, despite his own position as a deeply religious Hindu, not only dared to publicly avow his respect for all religions, especially Islam (and for which 'crime' he was assassinated by a fanatical Hindu), but also allowed the liberal politician, Nehru, and others, to establish a secular Indian state. One might wish that the rulers of modern theocracies would be endowed with that kind of sagacity, as, one hopes, would the religious militants everywhere in the world waiting to assume the mantle of state power. Equally, one may be entitled to hope that the leaders of liberal states in the world may have the wisdom to ensure that they do not, by their words or actions, allow the 'trivialization' of religion, under the cloak of the separation of religion and state. But more on this just a little later.

For the moment, let me draw (or, rather, redraw) attention to some remarks I made towards the end of Chapter 7. There I talked about 'Christian and Jewish liberals' and tried to explain how they tended to reconcile the conflict between their religious commitments, on the one hand, and their liberal ones, on the other. Earlier, in Chapter 5, we discussed Liberation theology and took note of the immense influence its message has exerted on believers, not only in Latin America, but elsewhere in the world also. While I clearly disagree about the extent to which, according to them, religion should be involved in social justice, or any other merely earthly preoccupations, I have to acknowledge that the very prevalence of this kind of thinking attests to the power of the two conflicting utopias and of the need for them to coexist. There clearly are, then, people around the world to whom my conclusion may appear to be preaching to the converted.

And beyond this circle, too, it should be deserving of attention by all truly reflective people, that is, those willing to lay aside their partisan loyalties, at least momentarily, in deference to the best interests of humanity at large. And I do hope that I have succeeded in making some sort of a case that a fruitful tension between these utopias does serve these best interests – not only generally, but even in the context of establishing a just social order.

Having now said a little about just who it is that, I suppose, could be interested in bringing about this fruitful coexistence – where it does not at the moment exist – and in ensuring its continuance where, happily, it already is in place, I now need to say a little about what precisely may be involved in bringing about this result. At the very least, it seems to me, it requires that nothing be done which has a tendency to close 'the public square', as Carter, and others before him, have suspected may be happening in relation to the religious voice. To quote Carter:

> The arena in which our public moral and political battles are fought has come to be called 'the public square', and Richard John Neuhaus in his well-known book *The Naked Public Square*, tells us that in America, the public square has become openly hostile to religion. I am not sure [he continues], that Neuhaus has it quite right – nowadays, religion is treated more as a hobby than as an object of hostility – but he and other critics are surely correct to point out that the rules of our public square exist on uneasy terms with religion.[8]

If it is, indeed, the case that the public square has either become hostile to religion, or even, as Carter prefers to see it, that the religious voice has been trivialized to the point of not being taken seriously, then, in the context of my recommendation certainly, something very unfortunate has occurred – whether it is in America only or anywhere else in the world!

Carter is candid in acknowledging that some of this trivialization of religion may be blamed on religion itself, especially on what he calls 'political preaching'[9] and what, following his line of argument, I might call instances of 'taking God's name in vain' – that is, when all sorts of trivial pursuits get bandied about as if they were God's pet causes. But insofar as this trivialization, or the hostility to religion, is a consequence of the intolerant atmosphere caused or encouraged by the successes of liberalism and its presuppositions, liberals surely must have an obligation to do everything they can to reverse the trend. For it must be against all the tenets of liberalism either to silence a voice because of its origins or laugh it out of the public square because it was religious in motivation. A liberal must, in my opinion, show respect for the dissenting voice, even while disagreeing with it, no matter where it comes from. If that message were not central to liberalism, I do not see what else could be! But that having been said, is there a similar obligation on the other side to provide for the free expression and respectful hearing of the liberal voice, or, for that matter, of any dissenting voice? I am afraid the answer has to be 'yes'. Religion may not have the credal advantage of liberalism in this respect, for it does entail firmly holding onto its own insights, truths or revelations. But a little humility on the part of the religious could help keep the public square open, without the abandonment of conviction. The believer does not have to pretend always to know when, in what form and through whose voice God may please to reveal His truths. And humility and true religiosity have always been excellent friends!

What else does this nurturing of coexistence imply? Respecting the separation principle – that is, the separation of religion and state (and of the politics of power) would also, to my mind, seem to be called for. The principle was, after all, devised to ensure, among other things, that the freedom to worship be given the same protection as the freedom not to worship and to hold non-religious, liberal, or other independent, views. And the best results for all concerned on this count, it seems to me, are obtained when this separation is respected, in letter and in spirit. A liberal state does, at least in principle, acknowledge this, despite failures in practice: at least, so it should. Would religious zealots, opposed to the principle, start recoiling from undermining it? I doubt it, although I think they should – wherever they happen to be!

How about the non-zealots? What I have to say to them may, I think, be best expressed in the following passage from Carter, again:

> The closer the religions move to the center of secular power (as against influence), the less likely they are to discover meanings that are in competition with those imposed by the state. The simple reason for this is that if the religions are able to impose their own meanings, there is no longer any distinction, and, thus, no longer important work for the triumphant religions as autonomous agencies to do. This abandonment of the role of external moral critic and alternative source of values and meaning will make sense when the Second Coming is at hand, but not before. Until that time, it is vital that the religions struggle to maintain the tension between the meanings and understanding propounded by the state and the very different set of meanings and understandings that the contemplation of the ultimate frequently suggests.[10]

Finally, I should add, perhaps, that, in my opinion, both religion and liberalism are here to stay; and it would be unwise for either side to indulge in wishful thinking about the demise of the other. We saw, in my introductory remarks to the book, that many nineteenth-century intellectuals thought that, with the rapid advance of science and technology, religion would die a quiet death. That has not happened. Likewise, it seems to me that, despite the recent resurgence of religion, liberalism is not going to disappear. The two opposing visions spring from different parts of the human heart or head, it seems to me; and each answers to a different set of longings of the complex human psyche. So instead of frittering away their energies conniving at the demise of the other, each utopia must learn to live with the other. Perhaps both sides should try to learn from this bit of wisdom expressed by a revered poet-saint of India: 'Have a critic live close by, even if you have to build a home and hearth for him: for he cleanses your character, without soap or water!'

References and Notes

INTRODUCTION

1. Ling, Trevor, *Karl Marx and Religion*, Macmillan, London, 1980, p. 119.
2. Juergensmeyer, Mark, *The New Cold War?: Religious Nationalism Confronts the Secular State*, University of California Press, Berkeley, 1993.

1. JUSTICE: A PRELIMINARY SURVEY

1. John Rawls, for example, regards 'justice' as a virtue of social institutions, or what he calls 'practices'. He uses the word 'practice' . . . as a sort of technical term meaning any form of activity specified by a system of rules which defines offices, roles, moves, penalties, defences, and so on, and which gives the activity its structure. See John Rawls, 'Justice As Fairness', in *Philosophy, Politics and Society*, Peter Laslett and W. G. Runciman (eds), Basil Blackwell, 1964, p. 132.
2. David Miller, *Social Justice*, Clarendon Press, 1976, p. 17.
3. Thus although individuals or societies may be spoken of as being just or unjust, in recent philosophy, justice is typically regarded as a virtue of social institutions. See Rawls, op. cit., p. 132.
4. As Rawls says, 'Amongst an association of saints, if such a community could really exist, the disputes about justice could hardly occur; for they would all work selflessly together for one end, the glory of God as defined by their common religion, and references to this end would settle every question of right'. Rawls, ibid., p. 142.
5. David Hume, *An Enquiry Concerning the Principles of Morals*, J. B. Schneewind (ed.), Hackett Publishing Co., 1983, p. 21.
6. Miller, op. cit., p. 25.
7. Aristotle, *Nicomachean Ethics*, excerpted in *Justice: Alternative Political Perspectives*, James P. Sterba (ed.), Wadsworth, 1980, pp. 18–19.
8. Miller, op. cit., p. 23.
9. Miller, ibid., p. 20.
10. This slogan is commonly referred to as the Socialist Principle of Justice, enunciated by Karl Marx and Friedrich Engels. For an explanation of this principle, see 'Justice under Socialism', by Edward Nell and Onora O'Niel, in Sterba, op. cit., pp. 200–10.
11. Hans Kelsen, *What Is Justice?*, University of California Press, 1957, pp. 11–17.
12. Kelsen, ibid., pp. 20–1.

2. PHILOSOPHICAL CONCEPTIONS OF JUSTICE

1. Aristotle, *Nicomachean Ethics*, excerpted in Sterba, James P. (ed.), *Justice: Alternative Political Perspectives*, Wadsworth, 1980, p. 21.
2. Aristotle, excerpted in Sterba, op. cit., pp. 21–2.
3. Ibid., p. 22.
4. Immanuel Kant, excerpted in Sterba, op. cit., p. 42.
5. Ibid., p. 44.
6. Ibid.
7. Ibid., p. 45.
8. Ibid., p. 46.
9. John Rawls, excerpted in Sterba, op. cit., pp. 49–50.
10. Ibid., p. 50.
11. Ibid., p. 52.
12. Sterba, ibid., p. 6.
13. John Stuart Mill, excerpted in Sterba, op. cit., p. 93.
14. Ibid., p. 104.
15. Ibid., p. 93.
16. John Stuart Mill, excerpted in Solomon, Robert C., *Introducing Philosophy*, Harcourt Brace Jovanovich, 1989, p. 686.
17. Hayek, F. A., excerpted in Sterba, op. cit., p. 10.
18. Friedman, Milton, excerpted in Sterba, op. cit., p. 10.
19. Nozick, Robert, excerpted in Sterba, op. cit., p. 156.
20. For an explanation of the 'proviso', see Nozick, in Sterba, op. cit., especially pp. 167–71.
21. Ibid., pp. 163–4.
22. Hobbes, Thomas, excerpted in Solomon, op. cit., p. 667.
23. Marx, Karl and Engels, Friedrich, quoted in Sterba, op. cit., p. 11.
24. Ibid., p. 195.
25. Ibid., p. 194.
26. Ibid., p. 198.

3. THE IDEA OF JUSTICE IN THE GREAT RELIGIONS

1. Keith, A. B., 'Righteousness (Hindu)', in *Encyclopedia of Religion and Ethics*, James Hastings (ed.), New York, 1919, Vol. X, p. 805.
2. Ibid.
3. Ibid.
4. *The Bhagavadgītā*, II, 48; VI, 29, *et al.*
5. Ibid., IV, 7–8.
6. Rhys Davids, C. A. F., *Buddhism*, p. 118, quoted by Thomas, Edward J., 'Righteousness (Buddhist)', in *Encyclopedia of Religion and Ethics*, op. cit., p. 778.
7. Thomas, op. cit., p. 778.
8. Ibid., pp. 778–9.
9. Ibid., p. 779.
10. Ibid.
11. Ibid.

12. Ibid.
13. *Lalit Vistāra*, VII, 128, quoted by Thomas, op. cit., p. 779.
14. *Vajracchedikā Sūtra*, quoted by Gungoren, Ilhan, 'A Buddhist View of Creating a Just Society', in *The Search for Faith and Justice in the Twentieth Century*, James, Gene G. (ed.), New York, 1987, p. 119.
15. Gordon, A. R., 'Righteousness (in the Old Testament)', in *Encyclopedia of Religion and Ethics*, op. cit., p. 780.
16. Ibid.
17. Jer. 9:24, quoted by Gordon, op. cit., p. 782.
18. Bourke, D. J., 'Justice Of God', in *Encyclopedic Dictionary of Religion*, Meagher, Paul Kevin; O'Brien, Thomas C.; and Aherne, Consulo Maria (eds), Washington, DC, 1979, Vol. F–N, p. 1956.
19. Gordon, op. cit., p. 781.
20. Ibid.
21. Ibid.
22. See Kelsen, Hans, *What Is Justice?*, Berkeley, 1957, p. 39f.
23. Ibid., p. 54.
24. Ibid., p. 55.
25. Ibid., p. 59.
26. Allen, W. C., 'Righteousness (in Christ's teaching)', in *Encyclopedia of Religion and Ethics*, op. cit., p. 784.
27. Matthew, V:43f, quoted by Kelsen, op. cit., p. 45.
28. See Kelsen, ibid., pp. 43–54.
29. Ibid., p. 63.
30. Ibid., pp. 67–72.
31. Sachedina, Abdulaziz, A., 'The Creation of Just Social Order in Islam', in *The Search for Faith and Justice in the Twentieth Century*, op. cit., p. 104.
32. *The Korān*, 4:135, quoted by Sachedina, op. cit., p. 101.
33. *The Korān*, 2:112, quoted by Sachedina, op. cit., p. 107.
34. Sachedina, op. cit., p. 108.
35. De Vaux, B. Carra, 'Righteousness (Muhammadan)' in *Encyclopedia of Religion and Ethics*, op. cit., p. 811.
36. Wemsinck, A. J., in *A Handbook of Early Muhammadan Traditions*, quoted by Sachedina, op. cit., p. 99.

4. SOCIAL JUSTICE AND THE PREDICAMENT OF RELIGION

1. Phillip Berryman, *Liberation Theology*, Pantheon Books, New York, 1987, p. 16.
2. 'John Paul Says Church Mustn't Accept Injustice', a 'special' report by E. J. Dionne Jr, *The New York Times*, Tuesday, 29 January 1985.
3. Reverend Peter Sammon, a Roman Catholic priest and pastor of St Teresa of Avila Church on San Francisco's Potrero Hill is quoted as having made these statements, in the *San Francisco Chronicle*, 23 May 1995, p. A6.
4. For an attempted definition of 'religion', see S. C. Thakur, *Religion and Rational Choice*, Macmillan, London (Barnes & Noble, NJ), 1981, Ch. 3.
5. Bruce A. Ackerman, *Social Justice in the Liberal State*, Yale University Press, New Haven and London, 1980.

6.   Religions have used somewhat different myths and 'rationales' for women's subjugation. The one referred to in the text is one of its Christian versions, and I owe the language used to my colleague, Martha Reineke, especially to her then unpublished paper, 'Embodiment: A Conversation with Simone de Beauvoir and Maurice Merleau-Ponty', October, 1984.

5. LIBERATION THEOLOGY AND SOCIAL JUSTICE

1.   Gutierrez, Gustavo, *A Theology of Liberation*, New York (Orbis Books, Mary Knoll), 1973, pp. 48–9.
2.   Bonino, Jose Miguez, *Doing Theology in a Revolutionary Situation*, p. 89, quoted by James, Gene G., 'Faith, Justice and Violence in Latin American Liberation Theology', in *The Search for Faith and Justice in the Twentieth Century*, Paragon, New York, 1987, p. 72. I am indebted to this excellent essay by Gene James in more ways than can be formally acknowledged.
3.   James, op. cit., pp. 75–6.
4.   Segundo, Juan Louis, *The Liberation of Theology*, New York (Orbis Books, Mary Knoll), 1976, pp. 139–40.
5.   Gutierrez, op. cit., pp. 175–6.
6.   Ellacuria Ignacio, *Freedom Made Flesh*, quoted by James, op. cit., pp. 73–4.
7.   Gutierrez, in *The Mystical and Political Dimension of Christian Faith*, quoted by James, op. cit., p. 74.
8.   Gutierrez, *A Theology of Liberation*, p. 205.
9.   Ibid., pp. 275–6.
10.   James, op. cit., p. 77.
11.   Gutierrez, op. cit., p. 228.
12.   Ibid., pp. 6–7.
13.   For a good and sympathetic account of the 'essential facts' about Liberation theology, 'the revolutionary movement in Latin America', see Berryman, Phillip, *Liberation Theology*, New York (Pantheon Books), 1987.
14.   Ibid., p. 187.
15.   Ibid., p. 192.
16.   Ibid., p. 193.

6. RELIGION, ECONOMIC DEVELOPMENT AND SOCIAL JUSTICE

1.   Stevens, William K., 'Gore Promises U.S. Leadership on Sustainable Development', *The New York Times*, 15 June 1993, p. B6.
2.   Berger, Peter L., *Pyramids of Sacrifice: Political Ethics and Social Change*, Allen Lane, London, 1976, p. 51.
3.   Ibid.
4.   Thakur, Shivesh, 'A Touch of Animism' in *Dialectics and Humanities*, No. 3–4/1976, pp. 157–8.
5.   Hirsch, Fred, *Social Limits to Growth*, Routledge & Kegan Paul, London, 1977, p. 167.
6.   Ibid., pp. 27–55.
7.   Ibid.

8. This phrase refers to the title of the book by Hirsch, op. cit.
9. Adam Smith as summarized by Coats, A. W. and quoted by Hirsch, op. cit., p. 137.
10. Mill, John Stuart, *Principles of Political Economy*, Penguin, 1970, p. 120.
11. Mill, John Stuart, 'Utility of Religion', *Collected Works, X*, University of Toronto Press, 1969, p. 415.
12. Kristol, Irving, quoted by Hirsch, op. cit., p. 137.
13. Sen, Amartya, quoted by Hirsch, op. cit., p. 139.
14. Hirsh, ibid., p. 141.
15. Berger, op. cit., p. 61.
16. Ibid., p. 32.
17. Hirsch, op. cit., p. 178.

7. MODERNITY, NATIONALISM AND RELIGIOUS FUNDAMENTALISM

1. Martin E. Marty and R. Scott Appleby, editors of *Fundamentalisms Observed*, University of Chicago Press, 1991, argue for the use of 'fundamentalism', pp. viii–ix, especially; but Mark Juergensmeyer cautions against that and prefers 'religious nationalism', in his *The New Cold War?: Religious Nationalism Confronts the Secular State*, University of California Press, 1993, pp. 4–8, especially.
2. *Webster's New International Dictionary*, 2nd edition, 1957.
3. See Juergensmeyer, op. cit., p. 4.
4. Marty and Appleby, op. cit., p. viii.
5. Ibid., pp. ix–x.
6. Juergensmeyer, op. cit., p. 6.
7. Ibid., p. 40.
8. Ibid., p. 190.
9. Evans-Prichard, E. E., *Theories of Primitive Religion*, Oxford, 1977, pp. 194–200.
10. Juergensmeyer, op. cit., p. 5. He cites Bruce Lawrence as using 'anti-modernism' to 'define fundamentalism as a global concept, for it suggests a religious revolt against the secular ideology that often accompanies modern society'.
11. Ibid., p. 5.
12. Ibid., p. 191.
13. Ibid.
14. Ibid.
15. Ibid., p. 187.

8. RELIGION, POLITICS AND PUBLIC LIFE

1. Thompson, Kenneth W., 'Religion and Politics in the United States: An Overview', *The Annals of the American Academy of Political and Social Science*, Vol. 483, January, 1986, p. 18.
2. Carter, Stephen L., *The Culture of Disbelief*, Anchor Books, New York, 1994, p. 1.

3. Ibid., p. 134.
4. Marty, Martin (and others), *Religion and Public Life*, Xavier University Press, Cincinnati, OH, 1986, p. 43.
5. Carter, op. cit., p. 82.
6. Mark XII:14ff., quoted by Kelsen, op. cit., p. 49.
7. Reichley, James A., *Religion in American Public Life*, The Brookings Institution, Washington, DC, 1985, p. 108.
8. See 'To What God . . . ?', in *The Experience of Religious Diversity*, John Hick and Hasan Askari (eds), Gower Publishing Company, Aldershot (UK) and Brookfield, VT (USA), 1985, pp. 119–30.
9. Carter, op. cit., p. 112.
10. Ibid. This phrase forms the title of Part I of Carter's book.
11. Marty, op. cit., pp. 44ff.

9. THE KINGDOM OF GOD AND THE 'GOOD LIFE' ON EARTH

1. Brown, John, Pairman, 'Kingdom of God', in *Encyclopedia of Religion*, Eliade, M. (ed.), p. 306.
2. Luke, 11:2, quoted by Gilbert, G. H., in *Encyclopedia of Religion and Ethics*, p. 736.
3. Mark, 12:34, quoted by Gilbert, ibid.
4. Mark, 9:1, quoted by Gilbert, ibid.
5. Price, James, *The New Testament: Its History and Theology*, Macmillan, New York and London, 1987, p. 176.
6. Schmidt, Werner H., *The Faith of the Old Testament*, The Westminster Press, Philadelphia, 1983, p. 149.
7. Ibid., p. 151.
8. Pannenberg, Wolfhart, *Theology and the Kingdom of God*, The Westminster Press, Philadelphia, 1969, p. 56.
9. Augustine, *City of God*, *xiv*, 28; excerpted in *The Essential Augustine*, Bourk, Vernon J. (ed.), Hackett Publishing Company, Indianapolis, 1978, p. 202.
10. Dillenberger, John (ed.), *Martin Luther: Selections from His Writings*, Anchor Books, New York, 1961, p. 370.
11. Calvin, John, in *A Compend of the Institutes of the Christian Religion*, Hugh T. Kerr (ed.), The Westminster Press, Philadelphia, 1964, p. 203.
12. Jer. 31:12, quoted by Gilbert, op. cit., p. 734.
13. Kant, quoted by Brown, op. cit., p. 310.
14. Basham, A. L., *The Wonder That Was India*, Fontana-Collins, 1967, p. 323.
15. Ringgren, Helmer, *Israelite Religion*, trans. by David E. Green, Fortress Press, Philadelphia, 1966, pp. 335–6.
16. Bhattacharya, Buddhadeva, *Evolution of the Political Philosophy of Gandhi*, Calcutta Book-House, Calcutta, 1969, p. 470.
17. Niebuhr, Richard, *The Kingdom of God in America*, Willett, Clark and Company, 1937, pp. 145–6.
18. *The Larger Sukhāvatī-Vyūha*, trans. by Max Muller, F., *Sacred Books of the East*, Vol. XLIX, Motilal Banarsidass, Delhi, 1972, 8.36–39.
19. Ibid., 8.26.
20. Ibid., 32.

21. Mark 10:25, quoted by Brown, op. cit., p. 307.
22. Luke 6:20, quoted by Brown, ibid.
23. Augustine, *City of God*, trans. by Walsh, G. G.; Zema, D. B.; Monahan, G. and Honen, D. J., Doubleday (An Image Book), NY, 1958, pp. 192–3.
24. *Sukhāvatī-Vyūha*, op. cit., 4.8.
25. Ibid., 8.10.
26. Ibid., 38.
27. See *St Thomas Aquinas on Politics and Ethics*, translated and edited by Sigmund, Paul E., W. W. Norton & Company, New York, London, 1988, p. 7.
28. Ibid., p. 8.
29. Ibid.
30. Shirazi, Sadra Al-Din (Mulla Sadra), quoted by Solomon, Robert C., *Introducing Philosophy*, Harcourt Brace College Publishers, New York, 1993, pp. 136–7.
31. *Sukhāvatī-Vyūha*, op. cit., 4.4.
32. See, for example, White, Lynn, 'The Historical Roots of our Ecological Crisis', in *Science*, Vol. 155 (1967), pp. 1203–7; reprinted in Barbour, Ian (ed.), *Western Man and Environmental Ethics*, Addison-Wesley, Menlo Park, CA, 1973.
33. Al Gore, quoted by Stevens, William K., 'Gore Promises U.S. Leadership on Sustainable Development Path', *The New York Times*, 15 June 1993, p. B6.
34. Schweitzer, Albert, *Indian Thought and Its Development*, trans. C. E. B. Russell, Adam and Charles Black, London, 1951.
35. Ling, op. cit., p. 101.

10. THE ETHIC OF RIGHTS AND THE ETHIC OF DUTIES

1. Kant, Immanuel, 'What is Enlightenment?', in *Foundations of the Metaphysics of Morals and What is Enlightenment?*, Beck, L. W. (ed.), Macmillan, New York, London, 1990, p. 83.
2. Sandel, Michael, *Liberalism and the Limits of Justice*, Cambridge University Press, 1984, p. 2.
3. Rawls, John, quoted by Sandel, op. cit., p. 176.
4. Sandel, op. cit., p. 178.
5. Ibid., p. 179.
6. Fishkin, James, *Justice, Equal Opportunity and the Family*, Yale University Press, New Haven, 1983, pp. 5–6.
7. Ibid., p. 4.
8. Ibid., p. 22.
9. Ibid., p. 32.
10. Ibid., pp. 35–6.
11. Sandel, op. cit.; Taylor, Charles, 'Cross-Purposes: The Liberal Communitarian Debate', in *Liberalism and the Moral Life*, Rosenblum, N. (ed.), Harvard University Press, Cambridge, 1989; Putnam, Robert, *et al.*, *Making Democracy Work*, Princeton University Press, Princeton, 1993 and Etzioni, Amitai, *The Spirit of Community: Rights, Responsibilities and the Communitarian Agenda*, Crown Press, New York, 1993.

12. Schuman, David, 'Our Fixation on Rights is Dysfunctional and Deranged', in *The Chronicle of Higher Education*, 1 April 1992, pp. B1–2.
13. Kant, Immanuel, *The Metaphysical Elements of Justice*, trans. by Ladd, John, Indiana University Press, Indianapolis, 1965, p. 45.
14. Ibid., p. 109.
15. Ibid., p. 113.
16. Kant, *Lectures on Education*, Prussian Academy Edition of Kant's works, 9:447–8. I owe this point (including the reference), and a lot more in this chapter to my colleague, William Clohesy.
17. Kant, *Religion within the Limits of Reason Alone*, trans. Greene, T. M. and Hudson, H. H., The Open Court Publishing Company, Chicago, 1934, p. 88.
18. Ibid., p. 89.
19. Ibid., p. 127.
20. Kant, *Foundations of the Metaphysics of Morals*, op. cit., p. 52.

11. CONCLUSION: THE CITY OF GOD AND THE CITADEL OF CREATURES

1. Waldron, Jeremy, 'Theoretical Foundations of Liberalism', in *The Philosophical Quarterly*, Vol. 37, No. 147, April, 1987, pp. 127–8.
2. Rouner, Leroy S., *Ethnic Conflict and World Community: Is There a Global Ethic?*, Alfred Stiernnotte Lecture in Philosophy Series, Quinnipiac College, Hamden, CT, 1992.
3. Sciolind, Elaine, 'At Vienna Talks, U.S. Insists Rights Must be Universal', *The New York Times*, 15 June 1993, pp. A1 and A6.
4. Ibid.
5. News report by AP, *The Waterloo Courier*, 1 September 1993.
6. See Aquinas, trans. Sigmund, op. cit., p. 8, for example. Such views about Hindu *mokṣa* or Buddhist *nirvāṇa* are so well known that they need no documentation.
7. Luther, in Dillenberger, op. cit., pp. 371–2.
8. Carter, Stephen L., op. cit., p. 51.
9. Ibid., pp. 67–82.
10. Ibid., p. 273.

Index

'good life' 101–3
  and environmental dangers 106–7
'good works' 73, 106
Gore, Al 107
greed 116
Greek influence on early Christian
  church 51, 53
Gṛhya sūtra 29
Gutierrez, Gustavo 51
  on faith 54, 57
  on Christian love 56
  on the political dimension 52–3
  on sin 55

hesed 34
Hinduism 29–31
  fossilized by pursuit of political
    power 95
  Hindu nationalism 85–6
  and the Kingdom of God 97,
    100–1
Hirsch, Fred 71, 72, 73
Hobbes, Thomas 26
Hopkins, Samuel 102
Hosea 37

ideal justice 8
ignorance 32
ijtihād 40
Imām 40
independence 18, 19
India
  Hindu nationalism 85–6
  religious nationalism 77
individual justice 9–10
individualism 94, 110, 113–14,
  115–16, 124–5
  counterweight to excessive 125
inequalities dictated by divine
  blueprint? 47
interdependence of the two utopias
  126–30
International Monetary Fund 79
Iran 77, 85, 94
Islam 39–41, 105
Islamic–Christian rivalry 79
  see also fundamentalism; religious
    nationalism
Īśvara 30

Jefferson, Thomas 84, 85
Jesus 36, 37–8
  Islamic view 39
  on the Kingdom of God 97–8
  on religion/state separation 91
John Paul II, pope 43
Judaism 34–6
  and the Kingdom of God 36, 97,
    98, 100
Juergensmeyer, Mark 82–3
just war 31
Justice
  conceptions of 15–28
  context 6–8
  idea of, in the great religions
    29–41
  kinds of 8–10
  and the Kingdom of God 99–100,
    105–6
  objects of 5–6
  primacy of 112
  principles of 10–11
  theories of 11–14
  'trilemma' of 114
  see also social justice

Kali Yuga 31, 97, 101
Kant, Immanuel 17–19, 110–11,
  112, 116–18, 120, 122, 124
  primarily a leader of the 'age of
    the Enlightenment' 120
karma 30, 32, 33, 118
karuṇā 33
Kaurava 30
ken 34
Khalifā 40
'kingdom of ends' 113
Kingdom of God 31, 36, 97–109,
  118, 120
  cognate concepts in Eastern
    religions 100–2, 104–5
  counterweight to excesses of
    liberalism 125
  Jesus's views 38–9, 97–8, 103
  and justice 99–100, 105–6
  and material wellbeing and
    happiness 101–3, 106
  transcendent state 97–9, 100,
    103